1 Discovering FRENCH Nouveau!

Bleu

Teacher's Edition

Lectures pour tous
with Test Preparation

McDougal Littell

A DIVISION OF HOUGHTON MIFFLIN COMPANY

Evanston, Illinois • Boston • Dallas

ISBN-13: 978-0-618-66118-3
ISBN-10: 0-618-66118-2   2 3 4 5 6 7 8 9 10 – VEI – 12 11 10 09 08 07
Internet: www.mcdougallittell.com

What Is *Lectures pour tous?*

A book that allows students to develop stronger reading skills by encouraging the use of a variety of comprehension and critical-thinking strategies.

Lectures pour tous, Level 1

Includes

- *Entracte* readings from Levels 1a, 1b, and 1 of *Discovering French, Nouveau!*
- Reading support throughout the selections
- A consumable format that allows students to mark up the text
- Vocabulary practice and enrichment
- Comprehension questions and short writing activities
- Additional literature for more reading practice and enrichment
- Academic and informational reading
- Test preparation models, strategies, and practice

Lectures pour tous, Level 2

Includes

- *Interlude* readings from Level 2 of *Discovering French, Nouveau!*
- Reading support throughout the selections
- A consumable format that allows students to mark up the text
- Vocabulary practice and enrichment
- Comprehension questions and short writing activities
- Additional literature for more reading practice and enrichment
- Academic and informational reading
- Test preparation models, strategies, and practice

Lectures pour tous, Level 3

Includes

- *Lecture* readings from Level 3 of *Discovering French, Nouveau!*
- Reading support throughout the selections
- A consumable format that allows students to mark up the text
- Vocabulary practice and enrichment
- Comprehension questions and short writing activities
- Additional literature for more reading practice and enrichment
- Academic and informational reading
- Test preparation models, strategies, and practice

The Interactive Reading Process

Lectures pour tous
encourages students to write in their books!

Lectures pour tous provides students and teachers with a unique resource that fosters reading comprehension. *Lectures pour tous* encourages students to engage or *interact* with the text. Activities before, during, and after reading a selection prompt students to ask themselves questions; clarify their ideas; and make personal connections—all thinking processes performed by proficient readers.

The following features help students interact with the text:

AVANT DE LIRE — **Reading Strategy** and **What You Need to Know** give students concrete ways to approach the selection, as well as the background knowledge and context necessary to understand it.

During Reading — **À réfléchir...** This feature appears at the key point of each reading and signals that students need to stop and answer the questions in the margins. These questions allow students to learn and practice a variety of reading skills and strategies, including

À réfléchir...

What other French expressions like **à la mode** do we use regularly in English? List a few here. How many others can you think of that have to do with food? **(Extend)**

- summarizing
- questioning
- predicting
- visualizing
- connecting
- clarifying
- evaluating
- drawing conclusions
- inferring
- stating opinions
- locating main ideas
- making judgments
- analyzing
- identifying cause-and-effect relationships
- understanding an author's purpose
- distinguishing fact from opinion

À MARQUER At specific points in each selection, students are directed to underline, circle, or highlight text that features key vocabulary or grammar concepts. In the *Lectures supplémentaires* section, students focus on one aspect of literary analysis and mark up the text accordingly.

Mots clés Vocabulary words that are key to understanding the reading are highlighted in bold and definitions are provided at the bottom of the page.

Reading Tip Useful, specific reading tips appear at points where language is difficult.

READER'S SUCCESS STRATEGY **Reader's Success Strategy** Specifically for struggling readers, these strategies are helpful for all types of learners. The strategies support those students who encode more easily through visuals, those who retain more easily through repetition, and those who just need a little extra help. In every selection, these notes give useful tips for comprehending vocabulary, context, concepts, and more.

Challenge These activities help students develop critical-thinking skills and encourage them to apply concepts beyond the printed page. The exercises actively engage students while highlighting the richness of the selections and literature.

Vocabulaire de la lecture Words boldfaced and defined in the selection are reviewed, requiring students to use the words contextually. Active vocabulary from the leçon appears in blue.

Tu as compris? Comprehension activities require students to use their understanding of the selection to extend their reading skills.

Connexion personnelle These brief writing activities help students connect the reading to their own lives.

Ongoing Assessment

In addition to increasing students' involvement in the reading process, *Lectures pour tous* offers you, the teacher, a window on students' progress and problems. Students' notes, responses, and other markings could be looked at regularly as part of the ongoing informal assessment process.

READER'S SUCCESS STRATEGY Make a Venn diagram and list all the body parts you know for both humans (**toi**) and birds (**les oiseaux**). Where the circles intersect, write the body parts we have in common with birds. Where they are separate, write the ones we don't share.

CHALLENGE *Alouette* is often used to teach children the names of parts of the body. What songs in English can you think of that do this? **(Connect)**

Inclusion in the Foreign Language Classroom

Making Reading More Accessible
Entractes and *Lectures supplémentaires*

French educators encounter a unique combination of students because of their objective of adding another language to the student's repertoire. Looking at an individual student's profile, there are those who are still learning how to read and those who read fluently in the same class.

Lectures pour tous includes more students before, during, and after they read through the enormous range of support and options. Students are reading to learn another language with the kind of accommodations that they need. Every student learns the same information, just not in the same way.

Before students read, they are given the critical background information they need so they are not reading the selection in isolation. These connections and critical background help students with the different cultural backgrounds and make no assumptions about what a student is supposed to already know.

While students read, they interact with what they are reading through point-of-use notes in the margins. Good readers apply certain strategies instinctively when reading. By making these strategies overt, more students can learn to use these strategies and, in turn, learn better reading habits.

Here are some of the features from *Lectures pour tous* that help students while they are reading.
- Reading Tips
- Reader's Success Strategies
- *À marquer*
- *Entracte* Readings on Audio
- *Lectures supplémentaires* on Audio
- *Mots clés*
- Challenge Activities

Lectures pour tous teaches students how to self-monitor, take notes, and apply new reading strategies when they encounter readings in classes, on tests, and in everyday life.

After the selection, the activities concentrate on vocabulary, comprehension, and personal connections. All three types of activities cement students' retention by developing their skills from controlled one-right-answer exercises to personalized open-ended critical thinking activities. This range addresses the broader range of students. Some students are more comfortable beginning with the bigger picture and then citing evidence; others are better at finding the details and then connecting those details to create the bigger picture. Ultimately, students could become comfortable going both from detail to world and from world to detail.

The more vocabulary students build through the rich assortment of readings, the better students are able to think critically and creatively. The use of graphic organizers helps students encode the information in two different ways: linguistically and visually. This helps with retention. Providing students with the opportunity to personalize their thoughts about the selection makes the selection stick. It has been encoded into their brain three ways: through words, through visuals, and through personalization. Therefore, they are much more likely to remember the selection. It has become meaningful to them even if they did not like it. The *Connexion personnelle* section of the reading gives the student the opportunity to say why.

Making Strategies More Effective
Academic and Informational Reading

This section of *Lectures pour tous* shares with students the unique strategies they need with each of these types of reading. Often students are asked to research, yet students do not know how to access different types of readings. This section is a sampling of the different types of tasks that students are asked to perform in school and on standardized tests:
• Analyzing Text Features
• Understanding Visuals
• Recognizing Text Structures
• Reading in the Content Areas
• Reading Beyond the Classroom

This array will develop students' strategies as well as serve as a resource so that when they come across a certain type of reading that they are unfamiliar with, they can see how to get the most out of the reading in the shortest amount of time.

Making Test Taking More Strategic
Test Preparation

The final section of *Lectures pour tous* features test preparation for reading, revising, editing, and writing. The section opens with general test-taking strategies.

Each type of test begins with an annotated model that shows students how to analyze the readings, the writing prompts, the direction lines, the questions, and the distractors, as well as work through standardized tests efficiently and effectively. The second step is for the students to practice with the same type of test. The final step is a self-check where students can verify their answers and self-evaluate areas where they may need more practice. This three-step process makes test-taking more transparent for students—demonstrating that it's not just a matter of a lucky guess, but that there are ways to make educated guesses.

This section shows students that once they learn and practice the strategies and avoid the pitfalls, they will be more confident when the *real* test takes place.

Making Students More Successful

At the end of the year, educators want students to walk out of the classroom knowing more than they did in September. Regardless of the level, students can progress. At right are general strategies for all levels of students. When a student can see his or her individual progress, that is when the student will be motivated to continue studying French.

Strategies by Student Group	
Strategies for Advanced Group Advanced students will be placed in accelerated classes in 9th grade and in Sophomore Honors, take the AP Language test (SAT-2) at the end of Junior year, and take the AP Literature test (SAT-2) at the end of Senior year. They will progress rapidly through the basics of the oral language and begin studying literature.	1. Involve students in a Pen Pal project to develop communication skills with peers in foreign countries. 2. Schedule meetings between Foreign Language and English teachers to develop common rubrics for literary analysis. 3. If taught in a heterogeneous class, substitute more challenging assignments for easier ones. 4. Make sure instruction is sufficiently complex and in-depth.
Strategies for Grade Level Group Grade level students are usually college-oriented, have an adequate foreign language reading level, but need lots of visuals for instruction.	1. Assess what these students already know and adjust the rate of introduction of new material based on frequent assessments during instruction. 2. Provide cumulative review of sound/symbol relationships, vocabulary and grammatical forms taught; use flash cards for class and partner review. 3. Progress through *Discovering French Nouveau!* at the recommended pace and sequence.
Strategies for Students with Learning Difficulties Group Learners have the lowest functional vocabulary level, are very visual learners, and need more cumulative review.	1. Assess what these students already know and adjust rate of introduction of new material based on frequent assessments during instruction. 2. Focus primarily on oral language. 3. Explicitly teach sound/symbol relationships, separating difficult discriminations in introduction. 4. Introduce vocabulary through drawings and personalize vocabulary. 5. Provide daily oral practice through group responding, partner practice, and short presentations.
Strategies for Students Needing Intensive Help (Special Education) Intensive needs students are those whose performance is two or more standard deviations below the mean on standardized measures. These students will probably be eligible for special education services. This is a very small percentage of the general population.	1. Determine reading level in English to guide the introduction of oral language content. 2. Follow the guidelines given for Students with Learning Difficulties. 3. Use a very visual approach and concentrate on oral language. 4. Directly teach sound-symbol relationships and vocabulary by clustering vocabulary words using sound-symbol relationship. 5. Place these students in lower grade level material if at all possible.

Chart written by Linda Carnine and Doug Carnine

Reaching All Readers

French teachers may find that the student who struggles to read and write in French is also a struggling reader in English. Improving a student's reading skills in English will also improve his or her success in the second language classroom. French teachers, like all teachers, may find it challenging to accommodate the wide range of reading abilities and interests among their students.

For those students who are hooked on reading, the challenge is to provide a steady diet of rich materials. But for many students, reading is a chore that requires enormous effort and yields little success.

Students who are not able to read at grade level often do not succeed in school. While much of the focus of the early grades is on learning to read, the focus shifts in the middle grades to reading to learn. Students who do not have a strong foundation in basic decoding and comprehension skills become struggling readers. Their poor reading ability denies them access to the content of the textbooks; as a result, they fall behind in almost every subject area. Below-level reading ability most often is the result of inadequate decoding skills, poor comprehension, or a combination of both.

Decoding skills provide readers with strategies for determining the pronunciation of the written word. Basic decoding skills involve matching letters and letter combinations with spoken sounds and blending those sounds into words. As students encounter longer—multisyllabic—words, they need to divide these words into manageable chunks or syllables.

Decoding is an enabling skill for comprehension. Comprehension is a process of constructing meaning from text. Readers integrate the information in the text with their prior knowledge to make sense of what they read. Specific comprehension skills and strategies, such as main idea, sequence, and visualizing, can help students recognize the relationships among ideas, figure out text structures, and create pictures of what they read.

Developing Fluency in All Readers

Reading fluency is the ability to automatically recognize words so that attention can be focused on the meaning of the written material. Fluency involves both decoding and comprehension skills; fluent readers decode text with little or no effort as they construct meaning from that text. Teachers can usually spot readers who struggle with decoding the text. Other readers, however, may be able to say the words and sound as though they are reading, but they have little or no understanding of what they read. These readers often go unnoticed, especially in the content areas.

Fluency is a developmental skill that improves with practice. The more students read, the better readers they become. The reading level at which a student is fluent is called his or her *independent reading level.* However, a student's independent reading level may vary with the type of material he or she is reading. For example, reading a short story is often easier than reading a textbook.

A key part in developing reading fluency is determining a student's independent reading level and then providing a range of materials at that level. Developing Fluent Readers on pages T10–T11 offers diagnostic tools for determining reading levels and tips for improving fluency.

Helping All Readers Break the Code

There are many reasons that some students struggle with reading. Often poor readers spend most of their mental energy trying to figure out, or decode, the words. With their brains focused on the letters and corresponding sounds, there is little attention left to think about what the words mean. Until readers achieve a basic level of automaticity in word recognition, they are not reading for meaning.

Although most students do have a knowledge

of basic phonics, some students fail to develop strategies for using the letter-sound correspondences. They often have difficulty decoding new words, and multisyllabic words are especially problematic. As students encounter longer words, they need to be able to break these words into parts.

Establishing a Reading Process

Good readers are strategic in how they approach reading. They consciously or unconsciously do certain things before, during, and after reading. Poor readers, however, often possess few or none of the strategies required for proficient reading. To help struggling readers, establish a routine for reading that involves strategies before, during, and after reading.

- **Before Reading** New ideas presented in reading materials need to be integrated with the reader's **prior knowledge** for understanding to occur. Have students preview the material to see what it is about. Discuss what they already know about the topic and have them **predict** new information they might learn about it. Talk about a **purpose** for reading and have students think about reading strategies they might use with the material.

- **During Reading** Good readers keep track of their understanding as they read. They recognize important or interesting information, know when they don't understand something, and figure out what to do to adjust their understanding. Poor readers are often unaware of these **self-monitoring strategies**. To help these readers become more involved in their reading, suggest that they read with a pencil in hand to jot down notes and questions as they read. If students own the reading materials, they can mark the text as they read. *Lectures pour tous* that accompanies *Discovering French, Nouveau!* is ideal for this type of work.

- **After Reading** Provide opportunities for readers to reflect on what they have read.

These can involve group or class discussion and writing in journals and logs.

Creating Independent Readers

As you work to give students the skills they need to read for themselves, you can also incorporate some basic routines into your classroom that will help your students extend their understanding.

- **Read aloud.** People of all ages love a good story. Read aloud to your students and hook them on some authors and genres they might not have tackled themselves. For most material, students' listening comprehension is more advanced than their comprehension of written material. Listening helps them develop the thinking skills needed to understand complex text.

- **Write daily.** Writing is a powerful tool for understanding. Encourage students to use writing to work through problems, explore new ideas, or respond to the literature they read. Encourage students to keep journals and learning logs.

- **Read daily.** Allow time for sustained silent reading. Set aside classroom time for students to read self-selected materials. Students who read become better readers, and students are more likely to choose to read if they can pursue ideas they find interesting.

- **Build a classroom library**. If possible, provide a wide range of reading materials so that students are exposed to diverse topics and genres. Respect students' reading choices. Struggling readers need first to view themselves as readers.

- **Promote discussion**. Set ground rules for discussion so that all opinions are heard. Model good discussion behaviors by asking follow-up questions, expanding on ideas presented, and offering alternate ways of viewing topics.

Developing Fluent Readers

Good readers are fluent readers. They recognize words automatically, group individual words into meaningful phrases, and apply phonic, morphemic, and contextual clues when confronted with a new word. Fluency is a combination of accuracy (number of words identified correctly) and rate (number of words per minute) of reading. Fluency can be taught directly, and it improves as a consequence of students' reading a lot of materials that are within their instructional range.

Understanding Reading Levels

Every student reads at a specific level regardless of the grade in which he or she is placed. Reading level in this context is concerned with the relationship between a specific selection or book and a student's ability to read that selection. The following are common terms used to describe these levels:

- **independent level**–The student reads material in which no more than 1 in 20-words is difficult. The material can be read without teacher involvement and is likely to be material students would choose to read on their own.

- **instructional level**–The student reads material in which no more than 2 in 20-words are difficult. The material is most likely found in school and read with teacher involvement.

- **frustration level**–The student reads material in which significantly more than 2-in 20 (or 89%) of the words are difficult. Students will probably get little out of reading the material.

If students read only material that's too easy, growth in skill, vocabulary, and understanding is too slow. If students read only difficult material, they may give up in frustration much too early.

Providing Reading Materials in the Student's Instructional Range

Most states have testing programs that provide information about each student's reading ability. Once you determine a student's general reading level, you can work with the library media teacher to identify reading materials that will be within the student's instructional level. To develop fluency, students should read materials that contain a high proportion of words that they know already or can easily decode. Work with each student to develop a list of books to read, and have students record their progress on a Reading Log.

Repeated Oral Readings

Repeated oral readings of passages is a strategy that improves fluency. Oral reading also improves prosody, which is the art of sounding natural when you read, or reading with appropriate intonation, expression, and rhythm.

Beginning readers sound awkward when they read aloud. They pause and halt at the wrong places; they emphasize the wrong syllables; they may read in a monotone. Repeated oral readings can increase fluency and prosody as students 1) identify words faster and faster each time they read; 2) correctly identify a larger percentage of words; 3) segment text into appropriate phrases; 4) change pitch and emphasis to fit the meaning of the text.

To improve fluency and prosody, select passages that are brief, thought provoking, and at the student's current independent level of reading. You may choose narrative or expository text, or have the student choose something he or she enjoys. Performing a play, practicing to give a speech, reading to younger students, and rereading a passage to find evidence in support of an argument are all activities that provide opportunities to reread. For the following exercise, you may choose to pair students together and have them read to each other, or use this as a one-on-one teacher-student or tutor-student activity.

1. Select an excerpt within the student's reading level.

2. Have the student read the passage aloud to a partner. The partner records the number of seconds it takes to read the whole passage, and notes the number of errors. Reverse roles so that each student has a chance to read to the other.

3. Read the passage aloud to the students so that students can hear it read correctly.

4. As homework, or as an in-class assignment, have students practice reading the passage out loud on their own.

5. After practice, have each student read aloud again to his or her partner, who records the time and the number of errors.

6. After repeated practice and readings the student will read the passage fluently, that is, with a moderate rate and near 100% accuracy.

Repeated Silent Readings

Having students silently read and reread passages that are at their instructional level also improves fluency. As they practice, students will recognize words more quickly each time, will group words into meaningful phrases more quickly, and will increase their reading rate. One nice thing about repeated silent reading is that a student can do it individually. Many students enjoy timing themselves when they read and seeing improvement over time. Have them keep a record on a piece of graph paper.

Modeling

Students benefit from repeated opportunities to hear French spoken fluently. By listening to live models or CDs, listeners can understand the rhythm of the language and the pitch and pronunciation of particular words and phrases. They can hear when to pause, when to speed up, and what words to emphasize. In addition, you can model or ask an experienced reader to read passages aloud. At most advanced levels, this technique is particularly useful to introduce students to various forms of dialect. As you play the CDs aloud, have students read along silently or chorally, or pause the CDs after each paragraph and have the students try reading the same passage aloud.

Phrase-Cued Text

Less proficient readers may not know when to pause in text. They may pause in the middle of a phrase, or run through a comma or period. They may not recognize verb phrases, prepositional phases, or even phrases marked by parentheses or brackets as words that "go together." This makes their reading disjointed and choppy, or gives it a monotone quality. Some poems have essentially one phrase per line and can be used to demonstrate to students how to phrase text. Or, you may take a passage and have students rewrite it with one phrase per line, so that they pause at the end of each line. Alternatively, you can show them how a passage should be read by inserting slash marks or blank spaces at appropriate places to pause. Choose passages appropriate to the students' reading level. Have students read and then reread the passage, stopping to pause at each slash mark.

Reciprocal Teaching

Reciprocal teaching refers to an instructional activity that teaches students concrete, specific, "comprehension-fostering" strategies they will need whenever they approach the reading of a new text. The activity consists of a dialogue between students and teacher, with each taking a turn in the role of the teacher or leader. Classroom use of this activity has been found to improve the reading comprehension of both good and struggling readers.

Step 1: Have everyone silently read a short passage (one or several paragraphs) of a new text. Model the following four thinking strategies using only the part of the reading that has been read.

- **Questioning** – Ask the class to think of a question that everyone can answer because everyone has read the same text. Model by generating a question for the class. Call on a student to answer your question. Ask that student to then generate a question for the class and to call on another student to answer her question. Repeat this procedure until you think all students are thoroughly familiar with the facts and details of the passage. (If students do not ask a question beginning with *why*, model one for them to move their thinking from literal to inferential comprehension.)

- **Clarifying** – Model for the class a confusion you need to clarify; for example, a word or a phrase that caused you to pause as you initially read the passage. Think aloud as you discuss your mental engagement with this section, explaining to the class how you figured it out. Ask students if they found any confusing parts when they read the passage. Have a dialogue about the problem-solving methods used by students to make sense of confusing parts.

- **Summarizing** – After students have comprehended the passage as a result of the reciprocal questioning and clarifying strategies, ask them to think of a one-sentence summary for the passage. Ask a volunteer to share his summary statement. Encourage others to revise, if needed, the shared summary by elaborating and embellishing its content. Identify the best summary through a dialogue with class members.

- **Predicting** – Now that students know what the first passage in the reading means, ask them to predict what the author will discuss next.

Step 2: Ask everyone to silently read another portion of text. Have a student volunteer repeat step 1, serving as the teacher/leader, over this new portion.

Step 3: In groups of four, have students silently read the next portion of text, taking turns role-playing the leader and following the four-step procedure.

Teacher's Role: Guide students' practice by monitoring the student dialogue in each group during steps 2 and 3. Remind students of the procedure and give additional modeling of the steps.

Reciprocal Teaching training provides students with explicit ways to interact with new text.

An ongoing review of all of the strategies provides a helpful reminder to students and encourages their pursuit of independent reading.

Strategies for Reading Copymaster

These comprehension and critical-thinking strategies can help you gain a better understanding of what you read. Whenever you find yourself having difficulty making sense of what you're reading, choose and use the strategy that seems most likely to help.

Visualize

Visualize characters, events, and setting to help you understand what's happening. When you read nonfiction, pay attention to the images that form in your mind as you read.

Cause/Effect

Try to figure out what will happen next and how the selection might end. Interpret the facts and infer the effects. Then read on to see how accurate your guesses are.

Compare/Contrast

Connect personally with what you're reading. Think of similarities and differences between the descriptions in the reading and what you have personally experienced, heard about, or read about.

Analyze

Question what happens while you read. Searching for reasons behind events and characters' feelings can help you feel closer to what you are reading. Look for patterns, hidden meanings, and details.

Synthesize

Review your understanding of what you read. You can do this by **summarizing** what you have read, identifying the **main idea**, and **making inferences**—drawing conclusions from the information you are given. Reread passages you don't understand.

Evaluate

Form opinions about what you read, both as you read and after you've finished. Develop your own ideas about characters and events.

1
Bleu

Lectures pour tous

with Test Preparation

Teacher's Edition

Bleu

1
Bleu

Discovering FRENCH
Nouveau!

Lectures pour tous
with Test Preparation

McDougal Littell
A DIVISION OF HOUGHTON MIFFLIN COMPANY
Evanston, Illinois • Boston • Dallas

Cover All photos by Lawrence Migdale/PIX/McDougal Littell/Houghton Mifflin Co.

ISBN-13: 978-0-618-77272-8
ISBN-10: 0-618-77272-3
Internet: www.mcdougallittell.com

1 2 3 4 5 6 7 8 9 10 – VEI – 12 11 10 09 08 07 06

Table of Contents

Lectures supplémentaires

Academic and Informational Reading 89

Test Preparation Strategies

Introducing *Lectures pour tous*

Lectures pour tous
is a new kind of reading text.
As you will see, this book helps
you become an active reader.
It is a book to mark up, to
write in, and to make your
own. You can use it in class
and take it home.

Reading Skills Improvement—in French *and* English

You will read selections from your textbook, as well as
great literature. In addition, you will learn how to understand
the types of texts you read in classes, on tests, and in the
real world. You will also study and practice specific strategies
for taking standardized tests.

Help for Reading

Many readings in French are challenging the first time
you encounter them. *Lectures pour tous* helps you
understand these readings. Here's how.

Avant de lire The page before each reading gives you
background information about the reading and a key to
understanding the selection.

Reading Strategy Reading strategies help you decide
how to approach the material.

What You Need to Know A preview of every selection
tells you what to expect before you begin reading.

Reading Tips Useful, specific reading tips appear at
points where language is difficult.

À réfléchir... Point-of-use, critical-thinking questions help
you analyze content as you read.

À marquer This feature invites you to mark up the text by underlining and circling words and phrases right on the page.

Grammaire As you read, this feature highlights key grammar concepts.

Vocabulaire This feature helps you with the new vocabulary as you read the selection.

Analyse littéraire This feature appears in the *Lectures supplémentaires* section and encourages you to focus on one aspect of literary analysis as you read.

Reader's Success Strategy These notes give useful and fun tips and strategies for comprehending the selection.

Challenge These activities keep you challenged, even after you have grasped the basic concepts of the reading.

Vocabulary Support

Mots clés Important new words appear in bold. Their definitions appear in a *Mots clés* section at the bottom of any page where they occur in the selection. You will practice these words after the selection.

Vocabulaire de la lecture Vocabulary activities follow each selection and give you the opportunity to practice the *Mots clés.* Active vocabulary words appear in blue.

Comprehension and Connections

Tu as compris? Questions after each selection check your understanding of what you have just read.

Connexion personnelle These short writing activities ask you to relate the selection to your life and experiences to make what you have read more meaningful.

Links to *Discovering French, Nouveau!*

When using McDougal Littell's ***Discovering French, Nouveau!,*** you will find ***Lectures pour tous*** to be a perfect companion. ***Lectures pour tous*** lets you mark up the *Entracte* selections as you read, helping you understand and remember more.

Read on to learn more!

Academic and Informational Reading

Here is a special collection of real-world examples—in English—to help you read every kind of informational material, from textbooks to technical directions. Why are these sections in English? Because the strategies you learn will help you on tests, in other classes, and in the world outside of school. You will find strategies for the following:

Analyzing Text Features This section will help you read many different types of magazine articles and textbooks. You will learn how titles, subtitles, lists, graphics, many different kinds of visuals, and other special features work in magazines and textbooks. After studying this section you will be ready to read even the most complex material.

Understanding Visuals Tables, charts, graphs, maps, and diagrams all require special reading skills. As you learn the common elements of various visual texts, you will learn to read these materials with accuracy and skill.

Recognizing Text Structures Informational texts can be organized in many different ways. In this section you will study the following structures and learn about special key words that will help you identify the organizational patterns:
• Main Idea and Supporting Details
• Problem and Solution
• Sequence
• Cause and Effect
• Comparison and Contrast
• Persuasion

Reading in the Content Areas You will learn special strategies for reading social studies, science, and mathematics texts.

Reading Beyond the Classroom In this section you will encounter applications, schedules, technical directions, product information, Web pages, and other readings. Learning to analyze these texts will help you in your everyday life and on some standardized tests.

Test Preparation Strategies

In this section, you will find strategies and practice to help you succeed on many different kinds of standardized tests. After closely studying a variety of test formats through annotated examples, you will have an opportunity to practice each format on your own. Additional support will help you think through your answers. You will find strategies for the following:

Successful Test Taking This section provides many suggestions for preparing for and taking tests. The information ranges from analyzing test questions to tips for answering multiple-choice and open-ended test questions.

Reading Tests: Long Selections You will learn how to analyze the structure of a lengthy reading and prepare to answer the comprehension questions that follow it.

Reading Tests: Short Selections These selections may be a few paragraphs of text, a poem, a chart or graph, or some other item. You will practice the special range of comprehension skills required for these pieces.

Functional Reading Tests These real-world texts present special challenges. You will learn about the various test formats that use applications, product labels, technical directions, Web pages, and more.

Revising-and-Editing Tests These materials test your understanding of English grammar and usage. You may encounter capitalization and punctuation questions. Sometimes the focus is on usage questions such as verb tenses or pronoun agreement issues. You will become familiar with these formats through the guided practice in this section.

Writing Tests Writing prompts and sample student essays will help you understand how to analyze a prompt and what elements make a successful written response. Scoring rubrics and a prompt for practice will prepare you for the writing tests you will take.

Entracte

Point-of-use comprehension support helps you read selections from *Discovering French, Nouveau!* and develop critical-thinking skills.

Reading Strategy
This feature provides reading tips and strategies that help you effectively approach the material.

What You Need to Know
This section provides a key to help you unlock the selection so that you can understand and enjoy it.

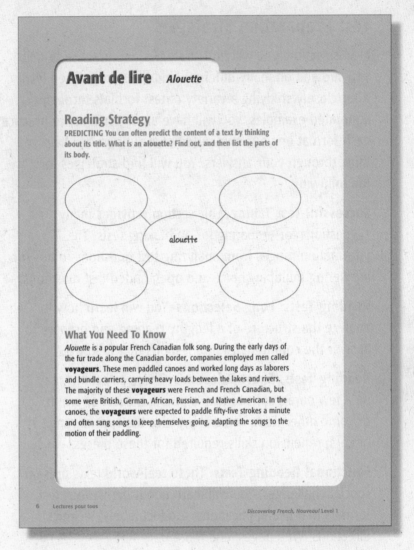

Avant de lire *Alouette*

Reading Strategy
PREDICTING You can often predict the content of a text by thinking about its title. What is an **alouette**? Find out, and then list the parts of its body.

alouette

What You Need To Know
Alouette is a popular French Canadian folk song. During the early days of the fur trade along the Canadian border, companies employed men called **voyageurs**. These men paddled canoes and worked long days as laborers and bundle carriers, carrying heavy loads between the lakes and rivers. The majority of these **voyageurs** were French and French Canadian, but some were British, German, African, Russian, and Native American. In the canoes, the **voyageurs** were expected to paddle fifty-five strokes a minute and often sang songs to keep themselves going, adapting the songs to the motion of their paddling.

6   Lectures pour tous

Discovering French, Nouveau! Level 1

Alouette

1. **A**louette, gentille **alouette,**
   Alouette, **je te plumerai.**

   Je te plumerai la tête,
   Je te plumerai la tête.

   5 Et la tête—et la tête
   Alouette—Alouette
   Oh oh oh oh.

2. Alouette, gentille alouette,
   Alouette, je te plumerai.

   10 Je te plumerai le **bec,**
   Je te plumerai le bec.

   Et le bec—et le bec
   Et la tête—et la tête
   Alouette—Alouette
   15 Oh oh oh oh.

MOTS CLÉS
alouette lark
je te plumerai I will pluck you
le bec the beak

À réfléchir...

Alouette is a song about plucking a bird's feathers, probably in preparation for eating. What other birds do people eat? **(Extend)**

A MARQUER **VOCABULAIRE**
Underline all the parts of the body that you recognize in the song.

READING TIP **Plumerai** is the future form of the verb **plumer**, *to pluck*. What English words might help you remember the meaning of the verb **plumer**?

À réfléchir...
Point-of-use questions check your understanding and ask you to think critically about the passage.

A MARQUER
VOCABULAIRE
This feature helps you with the new vocabulary as you read the selection. Underlining or circling the example makes it easy for you to find and remember.

MOTS CLÉS
Important vocabulary words appear in bold within the reading. Definitions are given at the bottom of the page.

Entracte *continued*

READER'S SUCCESS STRATEGY
Notes like this one provide ideas to help you read the selection successfully. For example, some notes suggest that you fill in a chart while you read. Others suggest that you mark key words or ideas in the text.

CHALLENGE
This feature asks you to expand upon what you have learned for enrichment.

Vocabulaire de la lecture

Mots clés

une alouette	*lark*	**les pattes**	*feet (of a bird)*
plumer	*to pluck*	**la tête**	*head*
le bec	*beak*	**le cou**	*neck*
la queue	*tail*	**le dos**	*back*
les ailes	*wings*	**gentil(le)**	*nice, sweet*

A. Label the parts of the **alouette's** body.

B. Match the verb on the left with the appropriate noun on the right.

_____ **1.** manger *(to eat)*   a. les ailes

_____ **2.** voler *(to fly)*   b. le bec

_____ **3.** marcher *(to walk)*   c. la tête

_____ **4.** penser *(to think)*   d. la queue

_____ **5.** se secouer *(to shake)*   e. les pattes

Unité 2
Alouette

9

Vocabulaire de la lecture
Vocabulary practice follows each reading, reinforcing the *Mots clés* that appear throughout the selection. Words that appear in blue are *leçon* vocabulary words in ***Discovering French, Nouveau!***

Tu as compris?
Comprehension questions check your understanding and provide the opportunity to practice new vocabulary words.

Connexion personnelle
These short writing activities help you see connections between what happens in the selection and in your own life.

Tu as compris?

1. Comment s'appelle l'oiseau?
   _____

2. Comment est l'alouette?
   _____

3. Quelles parties du corps *(body)* sont mentionnées?
   _____

Connexion personnelle

French Canadian fur trappers sang songs to keep themselves going. Do you know a song that keeps you going? Write two sentences like this:

J'écoute *(listen to)* la chanson *(song)* / musique _____.

_____

_____

_____

_____

Discovering French, Nouveau! Level 1

Lectures supplémentaires

Notes in the margins make literature from the French-speaking world accessible and help you read works by famous authors such as Jacques Prévert.

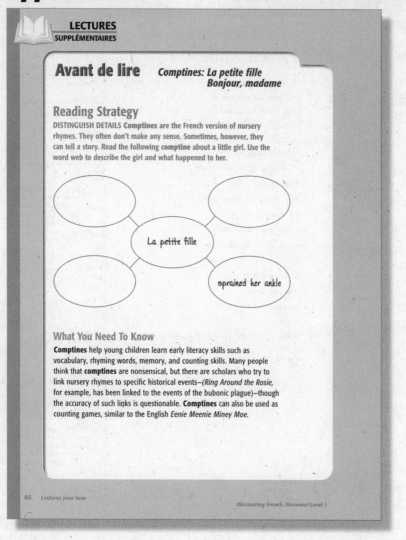

LECTURES SUPPLÉMENTAIRES

Avant de lire
Comptines: La petite fille
Bonjour, madame

Reading Strategy
DISTINGUISH DETAILS **Comptines** are the French version of nursery rhymes. They often don't make any sense. Sometimes, however, they can tell a story. Read the following **comptine** about a little girl. Use the word web to describe the girl and what happened to her.

La petite fille

sprained her ankle

What You Need To Know
Comptines help young children learn early literacy skills such as vocabulary, rhyming words, memory, and counting skills. Many people think that **comptines** are nonsensical, but there are scholars who try to link nursery rhymes to specific historical events—*(Ring Around the Rosie,* for example, has been linked to the events of the bubonic plague)—though the accuracy of such links is questionable. **Comptines** can also be used as counting games, similar to the English *Eenie Meenie Miney Moe.*

46   Lectures pour tous

Discovering French, Nouveau! Level 1

Reading Strategy
This feature provides reading tips and strategies that help you effectively approach the material.

What You Need to Know
This section provides a key to help you unlock the selection so that you can understand and enjoy it.

À réfléchir...

Cross out the statement that is *not* true about *La petite fille*. **(Clarify)**

The little girl is on a swing.

A man asks the little girl what her name is.

The girl's name is Juliette.

The little girl tells the man that a mischievous dog lives at 20, rue des Serins.

IIIÀ MARQUER▷ GRAMMAIRE
In *La petite fille*, underline the passage in which the man asks the girl what her name is. Then, write a sentence saying what your name is.

_____
_____
_____
_____
_____
_____

READING TIP In French, direct and indirect object pronouns come before the verbs. In *La petite fille*, find the sentence, "Un monsieur lui dit" and "je le sais bien." Note the indirect and direct object pronouns **lui** and **le**.

READER'S SUCCESS STRATEGY **Comptines** are meant to be said out loud. Read *La petite fille* out loud and notice where the rhyme scheme changes. Circle this line.

IIIÀ MARQUER▷ GRAMMAIRE

This feature asks you to notice how a particular grammar concept from the *leçon* is illustrated. Underlining or circling the example makes it easy for you to find and remember.

La petite fille

Une petite fille
sur[1] une balançoire
qui[2] se tord la cheville
et perd[3] la mémoire.

5 Un monsieur lui dit[4]:
«Comment t'appelles-tu?»
Elle répond: «Tant pis[5],
je ne m'en souviens plus[6],
est-ce que c'est Juliette
10 est-ce que c'est Juliane
est-ce que c'est Mariette
est-ce que c'est Mariane?
Mais ce que je sais[7],
je le sais bien:
15 Rue des Serins
numéro vingt
habite[8] un chien qui est **coquin**».

---
[1] on   [2] who   [3] loses   [4] says
[5] too bad   [6] I don't remember any more   [7] what I know
[8] lives

MOTS CLÉS
une balançoire swing
se tord sprains

la cheville ankle
coquin mischievous, a rascal

Academic and Informational Reading

This section helps you read informational material and prepare for other classes and standardized tests.

Academic and Informational Reading

In this section you'll find strategies to help you read all kinds of informational materials. The examples here range from magazines you read for fun to textbooks to bus schedules. Applying these simple and effective techniques will help you be a successful reader of the many texts you encounter every day.

89

VARIED TYPES OF READINGS

The wide variety of academic and informational selections helps you access different types of readings and develop specific techniques for those reading types.

SKILL DEVELOPMENT
These activities offer graphic organizers, Mark It Up features, and other reading support to help you comprehend and think critically about the selection.

Test Preparation for All Learners

Lectures pour tous offers models, strategies, and practice to help you prepare for standardized tests.

Reading Test Model
SHORT SELECTIONS

DIRECTIONS "Canada's Many Cultures" is a short informative article. The strategies you have just learned can also help you with this shorter selection. As you read the selection, respond to the notes in the side column.

When you've finished reading, answer the multiple-choice questions. Use the side-column notes to help you understand what each question is asking and why each answer is correct.

READING STRATEGIES FOR ASSESSMENT

Find the main idea and supporting details. Circle the main idea of the article. Then underline the details that support the main idea.

Use context clues. To discover what a "separatist" is, study the words and phrases around it. Which phrase helps define it?

Notice important details. Underline details that explain the importance of industry in Quebec.

Canada's Many Cultures

Canada's people come from different cultures, and many wish to safeguard their special language and customs. Some French-speaking Canadians are separatists, or people who want the province of Quebec to become an independent country. In 1980 and 1995, separatists asked for a vote on whether Quebec should become independent. Both times the issue was defeated, but the separatists promised to try again.

Quebec's Importance The federal government wants Quebec to remain part of Canada. Quebec is responsible for half of Canada's aerospace production, half of its information technology, and 38 percent of its high-tech industry. French culture is important in Canada's history and modern-day identity.

Laws Protecting Multiculturalism The Quebec provincial government has passed laws to preserve its citizens' French heritage. In an attempt to satisfy the separatists,

146 Lectures pour tous

Discovering French, Nouveau! Level 1

TEST PREPARATION STRATEGIES
- Successful test taking
- Reading test model and practice–long selections
- Reading test model and practice–short selections
- Functional reading test model and practice
- Revising-and-editing test model and practice
- Writing test model and practice
- Scoring rubrics

Revising-and-Editing Test Model

DIRECTIONS Read the following paragraph carefully. Then answer the multiple-choice questions that follow. After answering the questions, read the material in the side columns to check your answer strategies.

¹Paris, the capital of France. ²It is home to one of that nations cultural treasures—the Louvre museum. ³The building was constructed in the thirteenth century as a fortress. ⁴Then they opened it there in 1783 today it has over 500,000 square feet of exhibition space. ⁵The museum is located on a street called the Rue de Rivoli. ⁶Their are many famous works of art they're, including the Venus de Milo and the Mona Lisa.

READING STRATEGIES FOR ASSESSMENT

Watch for common errors. Highlight or underline errors such as incorrect spelling or punctuation, fragments or run-on sentences, and missing or misplaced information.

1 Which sentence in the paragraph is actually a fragment, an incomplete thought?
   A. sentence 1
   B. sentence 3
   C. sentence 4
   D. sentence 5

2 In sentence 2, which of the following is the correct possessive form of the word *nation*?
   A. nation's
   B. nations's
   C. nations'
   D. nations

ANSWER STRATEGIES

Incomplete Sentences A sentence is a group of words that has a subject and a verb and expresses a complete thought. If either the subject or the verb is missing, the group of words is an incomplete sentence.

Possessive Nouns In sentence 2, the word *nation* is singular. So, it takes the singular possessive form.

Writing Test Model

DIRECTIONS Many tests ask you to write an essay in response to a writing prompt. A writing prompt is a brief statement that describes a writing situation. Some writing prompts ask you to explain *what, why,* or *how.* Others ask you to convince someone of something.

As you analyze the following writing prompts, read and respond to the notes in the side columns. Then look at the response to each prompt. The notes in the side columns will help you understand why each response is considered strong.

Prompt A

Some child-rearing experts believe that young people should be kept busy after school and on the weekends with a variety of structured activities, such as music lessons, sports, dance classes, and so on. Others say that young people today have been "overscheduled" and need more time to themselves—to read, think about the future, and even just to daydream.

Think about your experiences and the way your non-school time is structured. Do you think lots of structure, more personal time, or a combination of the two is most beneficial to young people? Remember to provide solid reasons and examples for the position you take.

Strong Response

Today was a typical day for my little brother Jeff. He got up at five o'clock to go to the local ice rink for hockey practice. Then he was off to school. At the end of the school day,

NOTES

ANALYZING THE PROMPT

Identify the focus. What issue will you be writing about? Circle the focus of your essay in the first sentence of the prompt.

Understand what's expected of you. First, circle what the prompt asks you to do. Then identify your audience. What kinds of details will appeal to this audience?

ANSWER STRATEGIES

Capture the reader's interest. The writer begins by describing a typical busy day in his younger brother's life.

Avant de lire *Frère Jacques*

Reading Strategy

ACTIVATE PRIOR KNOWLEDGE Many words can have a double meaning. **Soeur** can mean both "sister," as in a relative, and "Sister," as in a religious nun. What word in the song can have a double meaning? Write the word and its meaning in the box.

Frère	can mean "brother," as in a relative, and "Brother," as in a monk (religious person)

What You Need To Know

In the 10th and 11th centuries, when monasteries played a crucial role in medieval culture, canonical time—or the times of day dedicated to prayer—influenced the development of our current understanding of time. **Matins** referred to the morning prayer time (although these prayers were originally observed when it was still technically night—around 2:00 A.M.). Water clocks were used to power the bells, **les matines**, that rang out prayer time, and the monks who had water duty were afraid of sleeping through their job. Around the year 1300, mechanical clocks were developed in order to provide greater accuracy, and these clocks provided the blueprint for the clocks we use today.

This reading can also be found on pages 122–123 of the Level 1 Pupil Edition. The audio is on CD 1, Track 1.

Frère Jacques

Frère Jacques,

Frère Jacques,

Dormez-vous?

Dormez-vous?

5 **Sonnez les matines.**

Sonnez les matines.

Din! Din! Don!

Din! Din! Don!

MOTS CLÉS

dormez sleep / are sleeping
sonnez ring

les matines the morning bells

Vocabulaire de la lecture

Mots clés

dormez *sleep / are sleeping*

sonnez *ring*

les matines *the morning bells*

un frère *brother*

vous *you*

A. Complete the song with the missing words.

_____Frère_____ Jacques,

_____Frère_____ Jacques,

_____Dormez_____ -vous?

Dormez-_vous?_____

Sonnez _les matines._____

_____Sonnez_____ les matines.

Din! Din! Don!

Din! Din! Don!

B. Fill in each blank with the appropriate vocabulary word.

1. _____Frère_____ Jacques dort *(is sleeping)*.

2. C'est le matin! _Sonnez_____ les matines!

3. Comment allez- _vous?_____

Tu as compris?

1. Comment s'appelle le Frère?

Il s'appelle Jacques.

2. Est-il français ou américain?

Il est français.

3. Qui est Jacques?

C'est un Frère.

Connexion personnelle

Imagine you are just meeting your tour guide, Jean-Luc, at the famous former monastery Mont Saint-Michel. Write a dialogue in which you greet him, introduce yourself, and find out his name. Ask him how he is doing.

—Bonjour, monsieur! Je m'appelle _____, et vous?

—Je m'appelle Jean-Luc.

—Comment allez-vous?

—Bien, merci.

—Au revoir, monsieur.

—Au revoir.

Avant de lire   *Alouette*

Reading Strategy

PREDICTING You can often predict the content of a text by thinking about its title. What is an **alouette**? Find out, and then list the parts of its body.

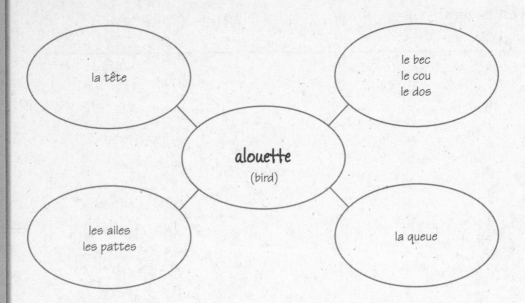

What You Need To Know

Alouette is a popular French Canadian folk song. During the early days of the fur trade along the Canadian border, companies employed men called **voyageurs**. These men paddled canoes and worked long days as laborers and bundle carriers, carrying heavy loads between the lakes and rivers. The majority of these **voyageurs** were French and French Canadian, but some were British, German, African, Russian, and Native American. In the canoes, the **voyageurs** were expected to paddle fifty-five strokes a minute and often sang songs to keep themselves going, adapting the songs to the motion of their paddling.

This reading can also be found on page 69 of the Level 1 Pupil Edition. The audio is on CD 2, Track 2.

Alouette

1. **A**louette, gentille **alouette,**
   Alouette, **je te plumerai.**

   Je te plumerai la tête,
   Je te plumerai la tête.

5 Et la tête—et la tête
   Alouette—Alouette
   Oh oh oh oh.

2. Alouette, gentille alouette,
   Alouette, je te plumerai.

10 Je te plumerai l**e bec,**
   Je te plumerai le bec.

   Et le bec—et le bec
   Et la tête—et la tête
   Alouette—Alouette
15 Oh oh oh oh.

MOTS CLÉS

alouette lark

je te plumerai I will pluck you

le bec the beak

À réfléchir...

Alouette is a song about plucking a bird's feathers, probably in preparation for eating. What other birds do people eat? **(Extend)**

turkey, pigeon, chicken, pheasant

_____

_____

_____

_____

_____

_____

▮▮▮À MARQUER▷ VOCABULAIRE
Underline all the parts of the body that you recognize in the song.

READING TIP Plumerai
is the future form of the verb **plumer,** *to pluck.* What English words might help you remember the meaning of the verb **plumer**?

plume, plumage

_____

_____

_____

CHALLENGE *Alouette* is often used to teach children the names of parts of the body. What songs in English can you think of that do this? (**Connect**)

Head, shoulders, knees and toes;
If you're happy and you know it.

Alouette

A - lou - et - te, gen - tille a - lou - et - te,
a - lou - et - te, je te plu - me - rai.
Je te plu - me - rai la tête, je te plu - me - rai la tête.
Et la tête, et la tête, a - lou - ett', a - lou - ett', oh!

3. Je te plumerai le cou...

4. Je te plumerai **les ailes**...

5. Je te plumerai le dos...

6. Je te plumerai **les pattes**...

20 7. Je te plumerai **la queue**...

MOTS CLÉS
les ailes wings   **la queue** tail
les pattes feet (of a bird)

Vocabulaire de la lecture

Mots clés

    une alouette *lark*

    plumer *to pluck*

    le bec *beak*

    la queue *tail*

    les ailes *wings*

    les pattes *feet (of a bird)*

    la tête *head*

    le cou *neck*

    le dos *back*

    gentil(le) *nice, sweet*

A. Label the parts of the **alouette's** body.

la tête

le bec

la cou

le dos

les ailes

la queue

les pattes

B. Match the verb on the left with the appropriate noun on the right.

  _b_ **1.** manger *(to eat)*   a. les ailes

  _a_ **2.** voler *(to fly)*   b. le bec

  _e_ **3.** marcher *(to walk)*   c. la tête

  _c_ **4.** penser *(to think)*   d. la queue

  _d_ **5.** se secouer *(to shake)* e. les pattes

Tu as compris?

1. Comment s'appelle l'oiseau?

Il s'appelle une alouette.

2. Comment est l'alouette?

L'alouette est gentille.

3. Quelles parties du corps *(body)* sont mentionnées?

les ailes, le bec, la tête, la queue, les pattes, le dos, le cou

Connexion personnelle

French Canadian fur trappers sang songs to keep themselves going. Do you know a song that keeps you going? Write two sentences like this:

J'écoute (listen to) la chanson (song) / musique _____.

J'écoute le rock.

J'écoute la chanson "Born in the USA."

Avant de lire   *Bonjour, Trinh!*

Reading Strategy

LOOK FOR COGNATES French words that look like English words and have similar meanings are called *cognates,* for example, **les maths** or **la permission.** Scan the reading for cognates and make a list here of the French words and their English equivalents.

FRENCH WORD	ENGLISH WORD
danser	dance
la musique	music
la guitare	guitar
un champion	champion
l'histoire	history
surfer	surf
chatter	chat

What You Need To Know

Collège is the equivalent of junior high or middle school, and includes the following levels: **sixième, cinquième, quatrième,** and **troisième**—the equivalents of sixth, seventh, eighth, and ninth grades, respectively. The curriculum for French **collèges** is standardized. Languages are given a high priority: Students take their first foreign language beginning in **sixième,** with four hours of class a week. Many students choose English as their first foreign language. In **quatrième,** students must choose their second foreign language, with three hours of class per week. Each student thus spends seven hours a week, for four years, studying a foreign language.

This reading can also be found on pages 122–123 of the Level 1 Pupil Edition. The audio is on CD 1, Track 3.

À réfléchir...

What do you and Trinh have in common? Make a list of your likes and dislikes. Where do you and Trinh share similar tastes, and where do you differ? (**Compare and Contrast**)

I...

play tennis, football, swim.
like to read.
don't like to play computer games.
like English, don't like math.
Trinh and I both like to play tennis and swim. We both like English and don't like math. Trinh likes to play computer games and I don't.

⫿⫿À MARQUER⟫ GRAMMAIRE

In this unit, you have learned how to use the verb **aimer** followed by an infinitive to say what people like and don't like to do. In the boxed text, underline all the sentences with **aimer** and an infinitive. Then, write three similar sentences below using **aimer** and an infinitive to say three things you like (or don't like) to do.

J'aime jouer au tennis.
Je n'aime pas jouer aux jeux vidéo.
J'aime nager.

_____

_____

READING TIP Remember that the verb **faire** is an irregular verb, meaning "to do or make." But **faire** is also used in many expressions like **faire un match, faire un voyage, faire attention.** Circle two expressions with **faire** that Trinh uses when discussing sports.

Bonjour, Trinh!

Bonjour!

Je m'appelle Trinh Nguyen. J'ai 14 ans. J'habite à Paris avec ma famille. Je suis élève de troisième au **collège.** J'étudie beaucoup,

5 mais je n'étudie pas tout le temps[1]. Voici ce que j'aime faire.

J'aime les boums parce que j'adore danser. J'aime la musique. J'aime **surtout** le rock, le rap et le reggae. J'aimerais[2] jouer de la

10 guitare, mais **je ne sais pas.**

J'aime les sports. En hiver je fais du snowboard et en été je nage et je joue au tennis. (Je ne suis pas un champion, mais je joue assez bien.) J'aime jouer au basket, mais

15 je préfère jouer au foot. Le week-end, quand il fait beau, j'aime faire du roller[3] avec mes copains.

J'aime mon collège. J'aime l'anglais parce

20 que le prof est sympa[4].

[1] all the time
[2] would like
[3] to go in-line skating
[4] nice

MOTS CLÉS
un collège   middle school or junior high
surtout   especially
je ne sais pas   I don't know / don't know how

J'aime aussi l'histoire, mais je n'aime pas trop[5] les maths.

À la maison, j'aime écouter mes CD de rock. J'aime aussi regarder la télé. J'aime le
25 sport et les films d'aventures.

> J'aime jouer aux jeux vidéo. Et, j'aime jouer aux jeux **d'ordinateur** sur l'ordinateur de ma mère mais avant, **je dois** demander la permission. J'aime surfer sur l'Internet et
> 30 **télécharger** de la musique. J'aime **envoyer** des mails à mes copains. Je n'aime pas chatter **en ligne** parce que je n'aime pas parler à des gens[6] que je ne connais[7] pas.

J'aime téléphoner à ma copine, mais je
35 ne téléphone pas souvent. (Mon père n'aime pas ça[8].) Et vous, qu'est-ce que vous aimez faire? Répondez-moi vite[9].

Amicalement[10],

Trinh

---

[5] too much	[6] people
[7] know	[8] that
[9] quickly	[10] In friendship

MOTS CLÉS
un ordinateur computer
je dois I must
télécharger to download

envoyer to send
en ligne on line

Unité 3
Bonjour, Trinh!
13

LES SPORTS	LA MUSIQUE
le snowboard	le rock
nager	le rap
le tennis	le reggae
le basket	
le foot	

LA TÉLÉ	L'ORDINATEUR
le sport	jouer aux jeux
les films d'aventure	surfer l'Internet
	télécharger de la musique
	envoyer des mails

CHALLENGE Do you think Trinh is someone you might like to get to know? Why or why not? **(Evaluate)**

Yes, I think I would like to get to know Trinh. He and I have a lot in common. We both like sports, and we both like English. He seems like an interesting person.

Vocabulaire de la lecture

Mots clés

un collège *middle school or junior high*

surtout *especially*

je ne sais pas *I don't know / don't know how*

un ordinateur *computer*

je dois *I must*

télécharger *to download*

envoyer *to send*

en ligne *on line*

habiter *to live*

étudier *to study*

faire *to do*

assez bien *well enough*

A. Fill in each blank with the appropriate vocabulary word.

Je suis élève au ___collège___. J'aime la musique, ___surtout___

le rock, le rap, et le reggae. J'aimerais jouer du piano, mais ___je ne sais pas___.

Je joue au tennis. Je ne suis pas champion, mais je joue ___assez bien___.

J'aime surfer sur l'Internet sur l'___ordinateur___ de mon père, mais

___je dois___ demander la permission. J'aime chatter ___en ligne___.

B. Match the verb on the left with the appropriate noun on the right.

___c___ **1.** télécharger   a. un match

___d___ **2.** envoyer   b. la ville

___b___ **3.** habiter   c. de la musique

___e___ **4.** étudier   d. un mail

___a___ **5.** faire   e. l'espagnol

Tu as compris?

1. Pourquoi est-ce que Trinh aime les boums?

Il adore danser.

2. Quelle sorte de musique est-ce qu'il aime?

Il aime le rock, le rap, et le reggae.

3. Qu'est-ce que Trinh aime faire en hiver? En été?

En hiver, il fait du snowboard. En été, il nage et il joue au tennis.

4. Pourquoi est-ce qu'il aime l'anglais?

Il aime l'anglais parce que le prof est sympa.

5. À qui est-ce qu'il aime téléphoner?

Il aime téléphoner à sa copine.

Connexion personnelle

Imagine that you are writing a response to Trinh's email. Using his email as a model, write and tell Trinh all about yourself. Be sure to write in French, and include your likes and dislikes.

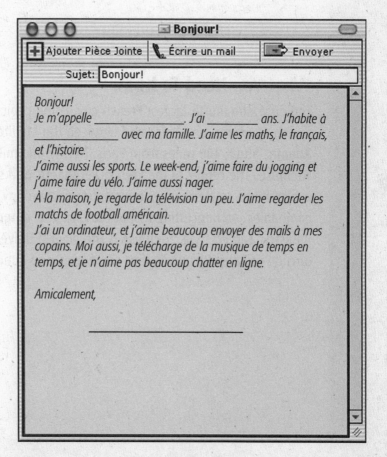

Avant de lire   *Bonjour, Brigitte!*

Reading Strategy

SCAN Reading very quickly to get a specific piece of information is called scanning. Scan the reading and complete the family tree. Include one detail about each family member.

What You Need To Know

Toulouse, the fourth largest French city, is the capital of the Midi-Pyrénées region of France, and is located between the Mediterranean and the Atlantic, about 400 miles from Paris. Nearly one million people live in Toulouse. The center of the French aeronautic and space industry, Toulouse is also home to electronics, information technology, and biotechnology companies. An interesting mix of old and new in terms of architecture, industry, and lifestyle, Toulouse is the biggest university town in France outside of Paris. Its universities serve over one hundred thousand students.

Bonjour, Brigitte!

Chers[1] copains américains,
    Je m'appelle Brigitte
Lavie. J'ai quatorze ans.
Voici ma photo. Je ne suis
5 pas très grande, mais je
ne suis pas petite. Je suis
de taille[2] moyenne[3]. Je
suis brune, mais j'ai
les yeux verts. Je suis
10 sportive. J'aime le ski,
le jogging et la danse
moderne.

    J'habite à Toulouse
avec ma famille. Mon
15 père travaille dans
l'industrie aéronautique.
Il est ingénieur. Ma
mère travaille dans une
banque. Elle est directrice[4]
20 du personnel.

---

[1] Dear   [2] size
[3] average   [4] director

MOTS CLÉS
les yeux eyes   **ingénieur** engineer
aéronautique aeronautical

À réfléchir...

1. Based on what you know from Brigitte's letter, which of the following items does she have? (**Clarify**)

   ☑ dog
   ☑ portable CD player
   ☐ television
   ☐ scooter
   ☑ computer
   ☐ compact stereo
   ☑ moped

2. Describe what you think Brigitte is like. (**Infer**)

   She is athletic. She has a lot of friends but doesn't have a boyfriend. She seems friendly and interesting.

À MARQUER ▷ VOCABULAIRE
In the boxed text, Brigitte describes her brother and sister and her dog, Attila. Circle the adjectives Brigitte uses to describe them.

READING TIP Notice all the different family members that Brigitte discusses. Underline all the ones that you see.

try to guess the meanings
of unfamiliar words before
you look at the English
equivalents. Often, the
context provides good hints.
Brigitte writes: "Je ne suis
pas très grande, mais je ne
suis pas petite. Je suis de
taille moyenne." What do
you think **taille moyenne**
means? Write the meaning
here:

medium size (height)

_____

CHALLENGE Use the Venn
diagram to compare the
things you have with the
things Brigitte has. Where
the circles are separate, write
in differences. Where they
intersect, write in similarities.
(Compare and Contrast)

toi

une mini-chaîne
un scooter

un ordinateur
un baladeur

une mob

Brigitte

J'ai une soeur et un frère. Ma petite
soeur s'appelle Élodie. Elle a cinq ans.
Elle est très mignonne. Mon frère s'appelle
Mathieu. Il a treize ans. Il est pénible. J'ai un
25 chien. Il s'appelle Attila mais il est très gentil.
(Il est plus gentil que[5] mon frère!) J'ai aussi
deux poissons rouges[6]. Ils n'ont pas de nom[7].

J'ai un baladeur et des quantités de CD.
Je n'ai pas de mini-chaîne. J'ai un ordinateur.
30 C'est **un cadeau** de ma marraine[8]. Je surfe sur
l'Internet et **j'envoie** des mails. Je n'ai pas de
scooter mais j'ai une mob.

J'ai beaucoup de copains, mais je
n'ai pas de «**petit copain**». Ça n'a pas
35 d'importance[9]! Je suis **heureuse** comme ça[10].

Amitiés,

Brigitte

_____

[5] nicer than	[6] goldfish	[7] name
[8] godmother	[9] It doesn't matter!	[10] like that

MOTS CLÉS

cadeau	gift	**petit copain**	boyfriend
j'envoie	I send	**heureuse**	happy

Vocabulaire de la lecture

Mots clés

les yeux *eyes*
aéronautique *aeronautical*
un ingénieur *engineer*
j'envoie *I send*
un cadeau *gift*

un petit copain *boyfriend*
heureuse *happy*
pénible *a pain*
mignonne *cute*
brune *dark-haired*
gentil *nice*

sportive *athletic*
grande *tall*
un baladeur *portable CD player*

A. Fill in each blank with the appropriate vocabulary word.

Chers amis,

Je suis à Paris chez mon oncle et ma tante. J'aime beaucoup mes cousines, ma

tante et mon oncle. Mon oncle travaille comme __ingénieur__ dans l'industrie

__aéronautique__. Mes cousines aiment les animaux, mais leur appartment est

petit. Elles ont un poisson rouge. C'est un __cadeau__ de ma tante. Ma

cousine Alice joue au tennis, fait du jogging, et en hiver, elle fait du ski. Elle est

__sportive__. Elle a un __petit copain__ qui s'appelle Pierre. Elle aime la

musique, et elle a un __baladeur__. Elle a un ordinateur et __j'envoie__

des mails à mes copains. Ma plus petite cousine a quatre ans. Elle a les __yeux__

bleus. Elle est très __mignonne__.

À bientôt!

Sophie

B. Match each word with its opposite.

__c__ **1.** triste   a. gentil

__d__ **2.** petite   b. pénible

__a__ **3.** méchant   c. heureuse

__e__ **4.** blonde   d. grande

__b__ **5.** sympathique   e. brune

Tu as compris?

1. Quel âge a Brigitte?

Elle a quatorze ans.

2. Quels sports est-ce qu'elle aime?

Elle aime le ski, le jogging, et la danse moderne.

3. Où est-ce qu'elle habite?

Elle habite à Toulouse.

4. Que fait le père de Brigitte? Sa mère?

Le père de Brigitte est ingénieur et la mère de Brigitte est directrice du personnel dans une banque.

5. Comment est sa soeur? Son frère?

Sa soeur est mignonne et son frère est pénible.

Connexion personnelle

Describe your best friend in the notebook.

Mon meilleur ami s'appelle Tom. Il est

très gentil. Il est assez grand. Il aime

la musique, surtout le jazz. Il n'aime

pas les ordinateurs.

Avant de lire   *Bonjour, Ousmane!*
                   MC Solaar

Reading Strategy

GATHER AND SORT INFORMATION One way to gain understanding of a text is to gather and sort information as you read. What kinds of music do you and your classmates like and listen to? Interview two people and fill out this chart. Then, use the chart to gather information about Ousmane.

Questions	Personne		Ousmane
	1	2	
Aimes-tu la musique?			oui
Quelle genre de musique préfères-tu?			le rap et le rock
Qui est ton chanteur/ta chanteuse préféré(e)?			MC Solaar
Joues-tu d'un instrument de musique? Lequel?			oui, de la guitare

What You Need To Know

Senegal, located on the west coast of Africa, was once part of French West Africa. It gained its independence in 1960. Bordered by Mauritania in the north, by Mali in the east, and by Guinea and Guinea-Bissau in the south, Senegal is just a bit smaller than South Dakota. While French is its official language, Wolof, Pulaar, Diola, and Mandinka are among several other languages spoken by the Senegalese. The capital of Senegal is Dakar, also the country's largest city, located at the westernmost point of Africa. Senegal is known for its music; its rhythms have inspired all kinds of music around the world, from jazz to blues to reggae.

À MARQUER VOCABULAIRE
Reread the boxed text. Circle the different types of music mentioned.

READER'S SUCCESS STRATEGY Compare and contrast the two descriptions of Ousmane and MC Solaar. Use the Venn diagram to organize your ideas. Where the circles are separate, write in differences. Where they intersect, write in similarities.

MC Solaar

- ses chansons ont beaucoup de succès
- donne des concerts dans beaucoup de pays

aime le rap

- est un peu musicien
- joue à des boums pour ses amis

Ousmane

Bonjour, Ousmane!

Bonjour! Je m'appelle Ousmane. J'adore la musique. J'aime surtout le rap et le rock. Mon chanteur[1] préféré est MC Solaar. Il chante très bien. J'ai beaucoup de CD de lui. Ma soeur,
5 elle, préfère le blues et le jazz.

Je suis un peu musicien. Je joue de la guitare. Et je ne joue pas trop mal. J'ai organisé[2] un petit orchestre[3] de rock avec des copains. Nous **répétons** le mercredi après-midi. Nous
10 ne répétons pas chez moi, parce que ma mère déteste ça[4]. Parfois[5], le week-end, nous jouons à des boums pour
15 nos amis.

[1] singer
[2] organized
[3] band
[4] that
[5] sometimes

MOTS CLÉS
répéter to rehearse

MC Solaar

le «Monsieur Rap» français

MC Solaar est né[6] à Dakar au Sénégal.
Il s'appelle en réalité Claude M'Barali.
Ses parents **émigrent** en France quand il a
six mois. Il **fait ses études** dans la région

5 parisienne. Après[7] **le bac,** il s'intéresse à[8] la
musique. Il compose des chansons[9] françaises
sur des rythmes de rap américain. Ses
chansons ont beaucoup de succès. MC Solaar
donne[10] des concerts en France, mais aussi en

10 Angleterre[11], en Allemagne[12], en Russie et dans
les pays[13] d'Afrique.

Aujourd'hui, MC Solaar est le «Monsieur
Rap» français! Dans ses chansons, il exprime[14]
des messages positifs contre[15] la

15 violence et pour la paix[16]. Voilà
pourquoi il est très populaire
en France
et dans le
monde[17]

20 **francophone.**

[6] was born	[7] after
[8] becomes interested in	[9] songs
[10] gives	[11] England
[12] Germany	[13] countries
[14] expresses	[15] against
[16] peace	[17] world

MOTS CLÉS
émigrer   to emigrate
faire ses études   to go to school; studies
le bac   short for **baccalauréat,** the exam at the end
   of **lycée** which guarantees university admittance
francophone   French-speaking

À réfléchir...

1. Which of the following is not true of MC Solaar? Cross it out. **(Clarify)**

He was born in Dakar, Senegal.

He sings in French.

He sings rap music.

~~His songs are often about violence.~~

He is very popular in France and in the French-speaking world.

2. Ousmane is a very popular Senegalese name. Why might France be a popular location to which Senegalese people would choose to emigrate? **(Infer)**

Many Senegalese might choose to emigrate to France because Senegal is a French-speaking country and there could be opportunities for them in France.

READING TIP Remember to look for cognates, words that look alike in English and in French. What cognates do you find in *MC Solaar, le «Monsieur Rap» français?* Underline them in the text.

CHALLENGE MC Solaar is originally from Senegal. He sings rap in French. What other musicians do you know who blend musical traditions?

Paul Simon, Ry Cooder

Vocabulaire de la lecture

Mots clés

répéter   *to rehearse*
émigrer   *to emigrate*
faire ses études   *to go to school; studies*
le bac   *short for **baccalauréat**, the*
   *exam at the end of **lycée** which*
   guarantees university admittance

francophone   *French-speaking*
jouer de   *to play (a musical*
   instrument)
un concert   *a concert*
la soeur   *sister*
la guitare   *guitar*

A. Match the verb on the left with the noun on the right with which it is best associated.

___*b*___ **1.** émigrer   a. l'école

___*c*___ **2.** jouer   b. un pays

___*a*___ **3.** faire ses études   c. le piano

B. Fill in each blank with the appropriate vocabulary word.

1. Sénégal est un pays __francophone__.

2. La fille de mon père et de ma mère est ma __soeur__.

3. J'adore la musique! Ce week-end, je vais à un __concert__ pour écouter de la musique.

4. Après le lycée, beaucoup de jeunes Français passent *(take)* un examen qui s'appelle le __bac__.

5. Ousmane joue de la __guitare__.

6. Pour bien jouer du piano, il faut __répéter__.

Tu as compris?

1. Quelle est la musique préférée d'Ousmane?

le rap et le rock

2. Quand est-ce qu'il répète avec ses copains?

le mercredi

3. Pourquoi est-ce qu'il ne répète pas à la maison?

parce que sa mère déteste ça

4. Où est né MC Solaar?

à Dakar, au Sénégal

5. Qu'est-ce qu'il exprime dans ses chansons?

des messages positifs contre la violence et pour la paix

Connexion personnelle

Who is your favorite musician?
Why?

Mon chanteur / Ma chanteuse

préféré(e) est...

Norah Jones

parce que...

j'aime bien le jazz

Avant de lire   *Les jeunes Français et la mode*

Reading Strategy

SKIM Before reading a long passage, it is helpful to read quickly to get a general idea of its content. Skim the paragraphs, noting clues that indicate the central theme or topic. By skimming, you can tell quickly what the reading is about. Then it will be easier to do a more careful reading. After skimming *Les jeunes Français et la mode,* write down some words or phrases that indicate what it is about.

la mode _____

le style _____

les jupes _____

les pulls _____

les vêtements _____

les jeans et les tee-shirts _____

What You Need To Know

Paris has long been a fashion center of the world. Rue du Faubourg Saint-Honoré is one of the most famous streets for connoisseurs of **haute couture.** It is lined with the boutiques of French designers, including Lanvin, Hermes, St. Laurent, Givenchy, and Cardin. For shoppers with a bit less money to spend, the **Grands Magasins**[1]–for example, Galeries Lafayette and Printemps, located on the boulevard Haussman–are a must-see. For savvy shoppers who are pinching pennies, **les soldes**[2] take place twice a year, once in winter and once in summer. During these times—one-month periods determined by the French government—all clothing stores put their merchandise on sale, and there are tremendous deals to be had.

_____
[1] department stores   [2] sales

This reading can also be found on pages 302–303 of the Level 1 Pupil Edition. The audio is on CD 1, Track 7.

Les jeunes Français et
LA MODE

Est-ce que vous aimez être à la mode[1]? Où est-ce que vous achetez vos vêtements? Et qu'est-ce qui compte[2] le plus[3] pour vous? le style? la qualité? le prix? Nous avons posé[4] ces questions à cinq jeunes Français. Voilà leurs réponses.

5

[1] in style   [2] counts
[3] the most   [4] asked

Florence (16 ans)

J'aime être à la mode. Malheureusement[5], mon budget est limité. La solution? Le samedi après-midi je travaille dans **une boutique de mode.** Là, **je peux** acheter mes jupes et mes pulls à des prix très avantageux[6]. Pour le reste, je compte sur la générosité de mes parents.

10

[5] unfortunately   [6] reasonable

MOTS CLÉS
une boutique de mode fashion boutique
je peux I can

À réfléchir…

1. Consider what you have learned about French young people and fashion. Do you and your friends share the same ideas with the French teenagers? Name some of the ideas you have in common and some ideas that are different. (**Compare and Contrast**)

My friends and I are concerned about fashion, too. Sometimes my mother buys clothes for me, but most of the time, I pick out my own clothes. I never sew my own clothes and I never go to fashion boutiques. Buying brand names is a bit like buying fashion designers.

To keep track of
what each of the French
teenagers says about buying
clothes, use a chart like the
one below. Highlight the
strategies each of the teens
uses to purchase clothes
or be in fashion, then write
them in the chart.

French Teenager	How he/she buys clothes
Florence	works in a fashion boutique and gets clothes at a discount
Chloé	sews ribbons and patches on clothes to create own style
Julien	goes to flea markets
Robert	waits for sales
Éric	mother selects clothes for him

READING TIP Spoken
language is different from
written language. Spoken
language can include slang
expressions—for example,
C'est marrant; C'est génial.
Sometimes, in spoken French,
the **ne** is dropped from a
negative expression, as in **C'est
pas cher** and **C'est pas drôle.**

Chloé (15 ans)

Pour moi, le style, c'est tout[7]. Hélas, la mode
n'est pas bon marché. Heureusement[8], j'ai une
15 cousine qui a une machine à coudre[9] et qui
est très adroite[10]. Alors, nous cousons[11] des
rubans[12] et des patchs sur nos vêtements. De
cette façon[13], nous **créons** notre propre[14] style.
C'est génial, non?

[7] everything	[8] fortunately	[9] sewing machine
[10] skillful	[11] sew	[12] ribbons
[13] manner, way	[14] own	

Julien (14 ans)

20 Vous connaissez[15] le proverbe: «L'habit ne
fait pas le moine*.» Eh bien, pour moi, les
vêtements n'ont pas d'importance. Avec mon
argent, je préfère acheter des CD. Quand j'ai
besoin de jeans ou de tee-shirts, je vais aux
25 puces[16]. C'est pas cher et c'est marrant[17]!

[15] know	[16] flea market	[17] fun

Clothes don't make the man.

MOTS CLÉS
   créer   to create

Robert (15 ans)

Aujourd'hui la présentation extérieure est très importante. Mais il n'est pas nécessaire d'être à la mode pour être bien habillé[18]. Pour moi, <u>la qualité des vêtements est aussi importante</u>
30 <u>que leur style.</u> En général, j'attends **les soldes.** J'achète peu de vêtements mais je fais attention à la qualité.

---
[18] dressed

Éric (12 ans)

Moi, je n'ai pas le choix[19]! C'est ma mère qui choisit mes vêtements. En ce qui concerne[20] la
35 mode, elle n'est pas dans le coup[21]. Elle achète tout sur catalogue et elle choisit ce qui est le moins cher[22]. C'est pas **drôle.**

---
[19] choice [20] as for [21] with it
[22] the cheapest (the least expensive)

ⅢÀ MARQUER **GRAMMAIRE**
You've just learned how to make comparisons. In Robert's section, underline an example of a comparison.

CHALLENGE Which student shares the attitude towards fashion that is closest to yours? Explain why. **(Connect)**

I am most like Robert. I also look for quality but I don't buy many clothes.

MOTS CLÉS
un solde sale   **drôle** funny

Vocabulaire de la lecture

Mots clés

une boutique de mode *fashion boutique*

je peux *I can*

créer *to create*

un solde *sale*

drôle *funny*

le prix *the price*

un pull *sweater*

bon marché *cheap / inexpensive*

génial *terrific*

cher *expensive*

acheter *to buy*

A. Fill in each blank with the appropriate vocabulary word.

1. Florence travaille dans une <u>boutique de mode</u>.

2. Le style de Chloé et sa cousine est <u>génial</u>.

3. Robert attend les <u>soldes</u> pour acheter ses vêtements.

4. Quand la mère d'Éric achète ses vêtements, il trouve que cela

   n'est pas <u>drôle</u>.

5. Selon ces jeunes Français, la mode n'est pas <u>bon marché</u>.

6. Puisque (*Since*) je suis riche, <u>je peux</u> acheter beaucoup
   de vêtements.

B. For each vocabulary word in the first column, find the sentence or phrase in the
second column that best describes it. Write the corresponding letter in the blank.

<u>c</u> **1.** une boutique de mode

<u>a</u> **2.** un pull

<u>d</u> **3.** cher

<u>e</u> **4.** le prix

<u>b</u> **5.** acheter

<u>f</u> **6.** créer

a. Je le mets quand il fait froid.

b. On paie avec l'argent.

c. un endroit où on peut acheter
   des vêtements

d. pas bon marché

e. ce qu'on paie pour quelque chose

f. faire

Tu as compris?

1. Comment est-ce que Florence gagne son argent?

Elle travaille dans une boutique de mode.

2. Qu'est-ce que Chloé fait pour être à la mode?

Elle met des rubans et des patchs sur ses vêtements.

3. Est-ce que Julien aime être à la mode?

Non, il n'aime pas être à la mode.

4. Est-ce que Robert achète beaucoup de vêtements?

Non, il n'achète pas beaucuop de vêtements.

5. Comment est-ce que la mère d'Éric achète les vêtements de son fils?

Elle achète ses vêtements sur catalogue.

Connexion personnelle

Imagine you are going on a trip to Paris. Make a list of the clothing items you might like to buy there. Include as much detail as you can.

une jupe noire en soie

un pantalon brun

une robe élégante

un costume

Avant de lire   *Le roller: un sport qui roule!*

Reading Strategy

PREDICT Use titles and pictures to predict what a reading will be about. What can you tell about this reading from the title and the picture on page 34? What will you be learning about in this reading?

Look at	Learn
Title	The selection will be about in-line skating.
Pictures	We'll learn vocabulary about in-line skating equipment.

What You Need To Know

In-line skating was first invented by a Belgian in the early 18th century, as a way to replace ice-skating in the summer. The first pair of in-line skates were nothing more than a pair of boots with wooden cylinders attached to the bottom in a single line. The design of roller skates was perfected in the 19th century by a Frenchman and later, an American, but it wasn't until the 1980s, when two hockey players—brothers by the name of Olson—found an old pair of in-line skates and decided to replicate the design and sell their skates under the name of Rollerblade, Inc., that the sport gained in popularity.

This reading can also be found on pages 354–355 of the Level 1 Pupil Edition. The audio is on CD 1, Track 8.

Le roller: un sport qui roule![1]

Beaucoup de jeunes Français participent aux sports d'équipe[2] comme[3] le foot, le basket et le volley, mais certains préfèrent les sports individuels comme le jogging ou la natation.
5 Aujourd'hui, beaucoup de jeunes pratiquent aussi les «sports de glisse[4]» comme le roller, le skate, la planche à voile (en été) et le ski et le snowboard (en hiver),

Le roller est particulièrement populaire
10 parce qu'il peut être **pratiqué** en toute[5] saison et par **les gens** de tout âge. Deux millions de Français font régulièrement du roller, principalement dans les grandes villes et surtout[6] dans la région parisienne.
15 «Pour moi,» dit Clément, 15 ans, «le roller est l'occasion[7] de me faire des nouveaux copains.» Mélanie, 17 ans, dit qu'elle fait du roller «parce que j'ai l'impression de vitesse[8], d'indépendance et de liberté. Je suis libre[9]
20 comme un oiseau.» Pour Charlotte, 21 ans, «le roller est un excellent moyen[10] de faire de l'exercice et de rester en bonne forme[11] physique.»

[1] rolls [2] team [3] like [4] gliding [5] any [6] above all [7] opportunity [8] speed [9] free [10] means [11] shape

MOTS CLÉS
pratiqué practiced **les gens** people

À réfléchir...

1. All of the following are mentioned as benefits of in-line skating except: (**Clarify**)

speed

saves money

doesn't pollute

~~competition~~

helps you stay in shape

2. Which of the following statements best summarizes the main idea of the reading? (**Main Idea**)

☐ In-line skating offers many advantages to someone who wants to stay in shape.

☐ In-line skating is a great way to get around cities.

☐ In-line skating is a fun but dangerous sport.

☐ In-line skating is a popular sport for many French young people which, when practiced safely, offers many benefits.

À MARQUER > **GRAMMAIRE**
Many adverbs in French end in **–ment,** as many in English end in –ly. In the boxed section, underline three adverbs and write them here along with their English equivalents.

particulièrement particularly
régulièrement regularly
principalement principally

L'équipement du roller!

le casque
(pour protéger la tête)

le protège-coude
(pour protéger les coudes)

le protège-poignet
(pour protéger les poignets)

les genouillères
(pour protéger les genoux)

les rollers

Pour certaines personnes qui habitent dans
25 les grandes villes, le roller est un nouveau
moyen de transport urbain. Philippe Tardieu,
un jeune avocat[12] de la région parisienne, va
à son bureau[13] en roller. «Le roller est plus
économique, moins polluant[14] et souvent plus
30 rapide que l'auto. Le roller, ça roule...!»

Le roller a beaucoup d'avantages, mais c'est
aussi un sport qui peut être dangereux si on
ne fait pas attention. Pour faire du roller, on

---
[12]lawyer   [13]office   [14]polluting

doit être en bonne forme physique et avoir

35 l'équipement nécessaire. On doit toujours porter un casque pour **se protéger** la tête. On doit aussi porter des genouillières pour se protéger les genoux[15] et des protège-poignets pour se protéger les poignets[16].

40 On peut faire du roller dans la rue ou sur toute surface **plane,** mais il est préférable de pratiquer ce sport dans les endroits réservés pour cette activité. Dans les grandes villes, il y a des «rollerparks» où les jeunes peuvent

45 aussi faire du roller acrobatique et jouer au hockey sur roller.

À Paris, une association sportive nommée Pari-Roller organise tous les vendredis soirs[17] une grande randonnée en roller dans les rues

50 de la ville. Cette randonnée[18] commence à dix heures du soir et finit à une heure du matin. Il y a souvent 12 000 (douze mille) participants de tout âge accompagnés de policiers en roller. Pendant cet **événement, les rues du circuit**

55 sont interdites[19] aux voitures. Pour beaucoup de Parisiens, cet événement est l'occasion de redécouvrir[20] leur ville dans une ambiance[21] **d'amitié,** de bonne humeur et de **fête** populaire.

---

[15] knees   [16] wrists   [17] every Friday evening
[18] long ride   [19] closed   [20] to rediscover
[21] atmosphere

MOTS CLÉS
se protéger to protect (oneself)
plane flat
un événement event
les rues du circuit roadways
l'amitié friendship
une fête festival

READER'S SUCCESS STRATEGY   Keep track of the reasons that different people have for in-line skating.

Clément can make new friends

Mélanie loves feeling free

Charlotte good way to get exercise and stay in shape

Philippe travels to his office— cheaper and pollutes less than a car

CHALLENGE. What kind of benefits might there be as a result of the Friday night in-line skating event in Paris? **(Infer)**

More people end up loving their city; they get to know other people in the city; might help keep crime down and foster good relationships between police officers and the people who in-line skate.

Vocabulaire de la lecture

Mots clés

pratiqué *practiced*

les gens *people*

se protéger *to protect (oneself)*

plane *flat*

un événement *event*

les rues du circuit *roadways*

l'amité *friendship*

une fête *festival*

faire du roller   *do in-line skating*

le soir *evening*

le matin   *the morning*

souvent *often*

A. Fill in each blank with the appropriate vocabulary word.

1. Le roller peut être dangereux. Il est important de ___se protéger.___.

2. Les randonnées du vendredi soir à Paris se passent dans une ambiance

   d'amitié et de ___fête___ populaire.

3. Pendant les grandes randonnées à Paris, les ___rues du circuit___ sont
   interdites aux voitures.

4. La randonnée à Paris est un grand ___événement___ pour la ville.

5. On peut faire du roller sur toute surface ___plane___.

6. Le roller peut être ___pratiqué___ en toute saison.

7. Les ___gens___ de tous les âges pratiquent le roller.

B. For each vocabulary word in the first column, find the phrase in the second column
that best describes it. Write the corresponding letter in the blank.

___c___ **1.** le matin

___d___ **2.** le soir

___a___ **3.** faire du roller

___e___ **4.** souvent

___b___ **5.** amitié

a. un sport actif pour tout le monde

b. le sentiment qu'on a pour ses copains

c. avant midi

d. après 6h

e. le contraire de rarement

Tu as compris?

1. Pourquoi le roller est-il particulièrement populaire parmi les «sports de glisse»?

Il peut être pratiqué en toute saison et par les gens de tous les âges.

2. Où va Philippe Tardieu en roller?

Il va à son bureau en roller.

3. Nommez deux choses qui sont nécessaires avant de pratiquer le roller.

On doit être en bonne forme physique et avoir l'équipement nécessaire.

4. Qu'est-ce qu'on peut faire dans des «rollerparks»?

On peut faire du roller acrobatique et jouer au hockey sur roller.

5. Combien de gens participent dans la grande randonnée à Paris tous les vendredis soirs?

Douze mille personnes participent dans la grande randonnée.

Connexion personnelle

What sport do you enjoy? Write down a sport that you like and list all its benefits.

Sport	Benefits
le ski	Il peut être pratiqué en hiver j'aime aller à la montagne on peut le pratiquer avec des amis

Avant de lire   *Bon appétit, Aurélie!*

Reading Strategy
SCAN Scan the list of pizzas on page 40 to see if there is one that a vegetarian might like to order. Write it here:

3 fromages; 4 saisons

What You Need To Know
The French have always been known for their food and particularly for **haute cuisine,** a style of cooking developed by Auguste Escoffier. **Haute cuisine** is characterized by the refinement of French techniques and the organization of professional kitchens into a hierarchy of **chef** and **sous-chefs,** an arrangement still typical of most restaurant kitchens today. In the 1970s, a new style of French cooking emerged—**nouvelle cuisine**—which emphasized presentation and the use of herbs and spices instead of the traditional reliance on heavier sauces. Today, French cooking in general is much simpler and emphasizes fresh, local ingredients **(cuisine de terroir).** A typical French meal might start with a hot or cold **entrée** (starter, or hors d'oeuvre), followed by soup, main course, salad, cheese, and dessert. Wine or mineral water is usually served. There is a greater influence of foreign cooking, too, today, because of the many immigrants to France, particularly from North Africa and Asia.

Bon appétit, Aurélie!

Nous avons demandé à Aurélie de décrire ses repas. Voici sa réponse.

À midi, je mange à **la cantine** de l'école et le soir à la maison. C'est ma mère qui fait les courses et c'est mon père qui prépare le dîner. Il adore ça! Il fait une cuisine assez
5 traditionnelle, mais bien équilibrée[1]. En général, on commence par une salade de **concombres** ou de tomates. **Ensuite,** il y a de la viande, par exemple, un bifteck ou du poulet, avec des haricots verts ou des pommes
10 de terre. Parfois, on mange du cassoulet[2] en boîte[3]. Après, il y a une salade verte et des fromages divers. Comme dessert, il y a du yaourt ou un
15 fruit. Avec le repas, on boit de l'eau minérale.

Quand mon père n'a pas envie
20 de faire la cuisine, on va au restaurant. Dans notre

[1] balanced   [2] bean stew with pork or duck
[3] canned

À réfléchir...

1. Based on what you know about Aurélie's eating habits, describe the ways in which your eating habits are similar to and different from Aurélie's. **(Compare and contrast)**

Aurélie and I both eat lunch in our school cafeteria. At home, my mother cooks dinner, but we don't always eat at the same time. We never eat cheese with our dinner. We rarely eat out in a restaurant. My friends and I love to eat pizza, too.

À MARQUER ▷ **VOCABULAIRE**
Reread the boxed section. Underline all the words that name a kind of meat, poultry, or vegetable.

READER'S SUCCESS STRATEGY When reading instructions or other texts that involve steps, look for words like **ensuite** and **après** that indicate chronological order.

MOTS CLÉS
la cantine cafeteria
un concombre cucumber

ensuite next

READING TIP Remember that in the United States, we use a different set of units for measuring both size and weight than many other countries, such as France, which use the metric system. If you look at the pizza menu, you'll notice that the size of the pizzas is given in **centimètres** (centimeters) instead of inches. Note, too, that the price is given in euros.

CHALLENGE Why do you suppose there might be more Vietnamese restaurants in France than Chinese restaurants? **(Draw conclusions)**

Vietnam is a former French colony, so many Vietnamese people already know how to speak French.

quartier, il y a un restaurant vietnamien que nous aimons bien. Mon **plat** préféré, c'est le riz avec des crevettes[4] et des petits pois.

25 Quand je sors avec mes copains, on va dans les fast-food. J'aime bien aller dans les pizzerias parce qu'on peut choisir ses ingrédients. En général, je prends une pizza avec du fromage, des olives et des **anchois.**

30 Avec la pizza, je bois souvent un soda.

[4] shrimp

ALLO pizza

MENU

		26 cm 1 pers	31 cm 2/3 pers	40 cm 3/4 pers
italienne	sauce tomate, origan, mozzarella, anchois, olives	7,50€	12€	15€
4 saisons	sauce tomate, mozzarella, crème, olives, tomates fraîches, champignons	7,50€	12€	15€
3 fromages	sauce tomate, mozzarella, origan, chèvre, Roquefort	8€	13€	17€
pescatore	sauce tomate, mozzarella, origan, oignons, saumon, champignons	8€	13€	17€
anglaise	sauce tomate, mozzarella, origan, bacon, oeuf, pommes de terre	9€	14€	20€
texane	sauce tomate, mozzarella, origan, boeuf épicé, pepperoni, oignons	9€	14€	20€

02-47-66-89-89

PETIT DICTIONNAIRE

frais / fraîche fresh
boeuf épicé spicy beef
oignon onion
champignon mushroom
origan oregano
chèvre goat cheese
saumon salmon

MOTS CLÉS
un plat dish / meal   **des anchois** anchovies

Vocabulaire de la lecture

Mots clés

la cantine *cafeteria*
un concombre *cucumber*
ensuite *next*
un plat *dish / meal*
des anchois *anchovies*
faire les courses *to go shopping*

faire la cuisine *to do the cooking*
la viande *meat*
du poulet *chicken*
des pommes de terre *potatoes*
du yaourt *yogurt*
le riz *rice*

A. Fill in each blank with the appropriate vocabulary word.

1. Chez Aurélie, c'est sa mère qui <u>fait les courses</u> et son père

   qui <u>fait la cuisine</u>.

2. À midi, Aurélie mange à la <u>cantine</u> de l'école.

3. Aurélie commence souvent son dîner avec une salade de concombres

   et <u>ensuite</u>, il y a de la <u>viande</u>.

4. Elle aime sa pizza avec du fromage, des olives, et des <u>anchois</u>.

5. Au restaurant vietnamien, le <u>plat</u> préféré d'Aurélie est le riz
   avec des crevettes et des petits pois.

B. Give an appropriate food item based on the description.

1. un oiseau qu'on peut manger <u>du poulet</u>

2. un légume qu'on mangeait tout le temps en Irlande <u>des pommes de terre</u>

3. on le mange froid, avec une cuillière <u>du yaourt</u>

4. un légume vert qu'on met souvent dans les salades <u>des concombres</u>

5. un petit grain blanc <u>le riz</u>

Tu as compris?

1. Où est-ce qu'Aurélie mange à midi?

Elle mange à la cantine de l'école.

2. Qui fait les courses chez Aurélie?

Sa mère fait les courses.

3. Qui fait la cuisine chez Aurélie?

Son père fait la cuisine.

4. Qu'est-ce qu'il y a comme dessert chez Aurélie?

Il y a du yaourt ou un fruit.

5. Quel type de restaurant est-ce qu'il y a dans le quartier d'Aurélie?

Il y a un restaurant vietnamien.

Connexion personnelle

Using the list of ingredients seen in the menu on page 40, plus any other French words you know, design your own personal pizza. Give it an appropriate name.

Ma Pizza: Méditerranée

Ingrédients:

sauce tomate, fromage, des artichauts,

de l'ail, des poivrons rouges, du chèvre,

des olives, et de l'aubergine.

Lectures supplémentaires

Lectures supplémentaires

In this section you will find literary readings in French. Like the **Entracte** readings, the literary readings have reading strategies, reading tips, reader's success strategies, critical-thinking questions, vocabulary activities, comprehension questions, and a short writing activity to help you understand each selection.

Avant de lire

Comptines: La petite fille
Bonjour, madame

Reading Strategy

DISTINGUISH DETAILS Comptines are the French version of nursery rhymes. They often don't make any sense. Sometimes, however, they can tell a story. Read the following **comptine** about a little girl. Use the word web to describe the girl and what happened to her.

is on a swing

doesn't know her name

La petite fille

knows that a mischievous dog lives at 20, rue des Serins

sprained her ankle

What You Need To Know

Comptines help young children learn early literacy skills such as vocabulary, rhyming words, memory, and counting skills. Many people think that **comptines** are nonsensical, but there are scholars who try to link nursery rhymes to specific historical events—*(Ring Around the Rosie,* for example, has been linked to the events of the bubonic plague)—though the accuracy of such links is questionable. **Comptines** can also be used as counting games, similar to the English *Eenie Meenie Miney Moe.*

La petite fille

Une petite fille
sur[1] **une balançoire**
qui[2] **se tord la cheville**
et perd[3] la mémoire.

5 Un monsieur lui dit[4]:

<u>«Comment t'appelles-tu?»</u>

Elle répond: «Tant pis[5],

je ne m'en souviens plus[6],

est-ce que c'est Juliette

10 est-ce que c'est Juliane

est-ce que c'est Mariette

est-ce que c'est Mariane?

Mais ce que je sais[7],

je le sais bien:

15 Rue des Serins

numéro vingt

habite[8] un chien qui est **coquin**».

---

[1] on	[2] who	[3] loses	[4] says
[5] too bad	[6] I don't remember any more		[7] what I know
[8] lives			

À réfléchir…

Cross out the statement that is *not* true about *La petite fille*. **(Clarify)**

The little girl is on a swing.

A man asks the little girl what her name is.

~~The girl's name is Juliette.~~

The little girl tells the man that a mischievous dog lives at 20, rue des Serins.

Ⅲ À MARQUER ⟩ GRAMMAIRE
In *La petite fille*, underline the passage in which the man asks the girl what her name is. Then, write a sentence saying what your name is.

_____

_____

_____

_____

READING TIP In French, direct and indirect object pronouns come before the verbs. In *La petite fille*, find the sentence, "Un monsieur lui dit" and "je le sais bien." Note the indirect and direct object pronouns **lui** and **le**.

**READER'S
SUCCESS
STRATEGY** **Comptines** are meant to be said out loud. Read *La petite fille* out loud and notice where the rhyme scheme changes. Circle this line.

MOTS CLÉS

une balançoire swing		**la cheville** ankle
se tord sprains		**coquin** mischievous, a rascal

The audio for this reading is on CD 1, Track 11.

À MARQUER **GRAMMAIRE**
In *Bonjour, madame,* underline
the passage in which someone
asks the woman how she is
feeling.

CHALLENGE What counting
rhymes do you remember
from your childhood that are
similar to *La petite fille* and
Bonjour, madame? How did
you use them? (**Compare and
Contrast**)

"One Potato"
"Black Shoe"
We used counting rhymes to
choose the person who would
be "It" in a game.

Bonjour, madame

— Bonjour, madame,

Comment ça va?

— Ça va pas mal.

Et votre **mari?**

5   — Il est **malade**

À la salade:

Il est guéri[9]

Au céleri.

[9] cured

MOTS CLÉS
   un mari husband   **malade** sick

Vocabulaire de la lecture

Mots clés

une balançoire *swing*

se tord *sprains*

la cheville *ankle*

coquin *mischievous, a rascal*

un mari *husband*

malade *sick*

une fille *a girl*

un monsieur *a man*

madame *title for an older woman (similar to Mrs.)*

un chien *a dog*

A. Fill in each blank with the appropriate vocabulary word.

1. La petite fille est sur une <u>balançoire</u>.

2. Elle <u>se tord</u> la cheville.

3. Le chien est <u>coquin</u>.

4. Un <u>monsieur</u> parle *(speaks)* avec la petite fille.

5. Le <u>mari</u> est malade.

B. List the **mot clé** that is the closest in meaning to the *opposite* of the word given.

1. un garçon <u>une fille</u>

2. bien <u>malade</u>

3. un chat <u>un chien</u>

4. monsieur <u>madame</u>

5. le poignet *(wrist)* <u>la cheville</u>

Tu as compris?

1. Où est la fille?

Elle est *sur une balançoire.*

2. Est-ce qu'elle sait *(know)* son nom *(name)*?

Non.

3. Où habite le chien?

Il habite *20, rue des Serins.*

4. Comment est le chien?

Il est *coquin.*

5. Comment est le mari?

Il est *malade.*

Connexion personnelle

Imagine that you are on a trip to France. Write out a dialogue in which you meet another person. Introduce yourself and ask that person's name and how he or she is doing. Find out how old he or she is. Give the replies. Use dashes to indicate a change in speaker.

— Bonjour! Je m'appelle

Anne. Comment t'appelles-tu?

— Je m'appelle Yves.

— Comment ça va?

— Ça va bien. Et toi?

— Ça va.

— Quel âge as-tu?

— J'ai quatorze ans.

Avant de lire   *Savez-vous planter les choux?*
Comptines: Bonjour
Les saisons

Reading Strategy

SCAN Scan the **comptines** for familiar words. Which words do you recognize? Write them here. What do they help you figure out about the **comptines**?

Savez-vous planter les choux: Doigts, pied, mains (parts of the body).
Planter (a cognate meaning to plant). The song is about planting something
with different parts of the body.

Bonjour: Madame, the days of the week. The **comptine** is a conversation
between women named for the days of the week.

Les saisons: The seasons. The **comptine** is about the changing of the
seasons.

What You Need To Know

À la mode is a French term meaning *fashionable* or *chic.* Its original meaning, when found in the phrase, **à la mode de** ____, means *in the manner of* ____, and usually refers to a country or other place. In the United States, we use the term **à la mode** most often to mean *with ice cream* and it usually refers to apple pie served with vanilla ice cream. This American use was coined in the late 19th century by a diner in New York and made famous by a reporter in the *New York Sun.*

À réfléchir...

What other French expressions like **à la mode** do we use regularly in English? List a few here. How many others can you think of that have to do with food? **(Extend)**

FOOD: à la carte, du jour, au gratin, au jus

OTHERS: bon voyage, RSVP, c'est la vie, coup d'état, déjà vu

READING TIP Nouns in French can sometimes be replaced by an object pronoun. In the song *Savez-vous planter les choux?*, notice the repeated line "on les plante". The object pronoun **les** refers to **les choux.**

READER'S SUCCESS STRATEGY Remember to read **comptines** out loud. *Savez-vous planter les choux?* is a song. Search the internet to get the music that goes along with the lyrics, and learn to sing the song.

Savez-vous planter les choux?

Savez-vous[1] **planter les choux?**
À la mode, à la mode,
Savez-vous planter les choux?
À la mode de chez nous[2]?

5 On les plante avec le doigt
À la mode, à la mode,
On les plante avec le doigt
À la mode de chez nous.

Savez-vous planter les choux?
10 À la mode, à la mode,
Savez-vous planter les choux?
À la mode de chez nous?

On les plante avec les mains…

On les plante avec le pied…

15 On les plante avec le coude…

On les plante avec le nez…

[1] Do you know
[2] our place / where we live

MOTS CLÉS
planter to plant   **les choux** cabbage

Bonjour

Bonjour, Madame Lundi,

comment va Madame Mardi?

— Très bien, Madame Mercredi;

dites[3] à Madame Jeudi

5 de **venir** vendredi

  danser samedi

  dans **la salle** de Dimanche.

[3] tell

Les saisons

Au printemps, p'tites[4] **feuilles**

En été, grandes[5] feuilles

En automne, plein d'[6]feuilles

En hiver, plus d'[7]feuilles.

[4] little   [5] big
[6] plenty of   [7] no more

MOTS CLÉS
venir to come	**la salle** room
danser to dance	**les feuilles** leaves

À MARQUER > VOCABULAIRE

In *Bonjour,* underline all the days of the week. In *Les Saisons,* underline the names of all the seasons.

_____

_____

_____

_____

CHALLENGE In *Les Saisons,* leaves are used as a symbol for the changing of the seasons. What else might you use to represent the passage of time? **(Extend)**

The sun and changes in temperature; ages of children; colors of earth, fields and gardens.

_____

_____

_____

_____

_____

_____

_____

_____

Lectures supplémentaires
Savez-vous planter les choux? /
Bonjour / Les saisons   **53**

Vocabulaire de la lecture

Mots clés

planter *to plant*	**les feuilles** *leaves*
les choux *cabbage*	**le printemps** *the spring*
venir *to come*	**l'été** *the summer*
danser *to dance*	**l'automne** *the fall*
la salle *room*	**l'hiver** *the winter*

A. Match the word on the left with the appropriate phrase on the right.

___b___ **1.** le printemps   a. il neige

___c___ **2.** l'été   b. mars, avril, mai

___d___ **3.** l'automne   c. il fait très chaud

___a___ **4.** l'hiver   d. octobre, novembre

B. Fill in each blank with the appropriate vocabulary word.

1. Madame Lundi, Madame Mardi, Madame Mercredi, et Madame Jeudi

vont *(are going to)* ___danser___ samedi.

2. Elles vont danser dans la ___salle___ de Dimanche.

3. On plante les ___choux___.

4. En été, il y a de grandes ___feuilles___.

5. Madame Jeudi va *(is going to)* ___venir___ vendredi.

6. On peut *(can)* ___planter___ les choux avec le doigt.

Tu as compris?

1. Quelles parties du corps sont mentionées?

le doigt, les mains, le pied, le coude, le nez

2. Qui va danser?

Madame Lundi, Madame Mardi, Madame Mercredi, Madame Jeudi

3. Où vont-elles danser?

dans la salle de Dimanche

4. Qu'est-ce qu'on plante?

les choux

5. En automne, est-ce qu'il y a plein de feuilles, ou plus de feuilles?

plein de feuilles

Connexion personnelle

If you could write your own **comptine,** what might you write about? In the center of the web, write a subject for your **comptine.** Then brainstorm words you might associate with it.

Avant de lire
Sur le pont d'Avignon
La terre

Reading Strategy

PREDICT Look at the titles of the two short readings–the song *Sur le pont d'Avignon* and the poem *La terre.* Based on the titles, what do you think the readings will be about? Write your predictions in the following chart.

Sur le pont d'Avignon	The song will be about (a bridge in) the city of Avignon.
La terre	The poem will be about the earth.

What You Need To Know

The famous Avignon Bridge–or the bridge of St. Bénezet–was the first bridge to span the Rhône River, the dividing line between France and the Holy Roman Empire. Nearby, in Avignon, is the Popes' Palace.

Jacques Prévert, the author of *La terre,* was a French poet and screenwriter who lived from 1900–1977.

Sur le pont d'Avignon

Sur[1] **le pont** d'Avignon

L'on[2] y danse, l'on y danse,

Sur le pont d'Avignon

L'on y danse tout en rond[3].

5 Les beaux **messieurs** font comme ça[4]

Et puis encore[5] comme ça.

Sur le pont d'Avignon

L'on y danse tout en rond.

Sur le pont d'Avignon

10 L'on y danse, l'on y danse,

Sur le pont d'Avignon

L'on y danse tout en rond.

Les belles **dames** font comme ça

Et puis encore comme ça.

15 Sur le pont d'Avignon

L'on y danse tout en rond.

Les officiers font comme ça

Les bébés font comme ça

Les bons **amis** font comme ça

20 Les musiciens font comme ça

---

[1] on   [2] people   [3] in a circle
[4] like that   [5] then again

À réfléchir...

Sur le pont d'Avignon is a children's song. What English songs about bridges do you know? **(Compare and Contrast)**

London Bridge

_____

_____

_____

_____

READING TIP In many children's songs and poems, repetition is used to help foster understanding. Underline the repeated phrases in *Sur le pont d'Avignon.*

READER'S SUCCESS STRATEGY Don't worry if you can't understand every word in the song and poem. Read for the gist and for overall understanding. Use the words you do understand to help you with what you don't understand. Find a few words in the reading that you already know, or which you can understand because they look like English words, and write them here.

danse

aime

amis

officiers

musiciens

bébés

MOTS CLÉS

le pont the bridge	**les dames** ladies
les messieurs gentlemen	**les amis** friends

LECTURES SUPPLÉMENTAIRES

À réfléchir...

In the poem *La terre,* why does the sun shine? **(Clarify)**

The sun shines for the earth, because the sun thinks the earth is beautiful.

ANALYSE LITTÉRAIRE Personification is a figure of speech that gives human characteristics to an inanimate object, or to an animal, or an idea. What is being personified in the poem *La terre?* Underline all the words that are being given human characteristics.

CHALLENGE How might you describe the behavior of the earth in the poem *La terre?* **(INFER)**

The earth is acting flirty—turning so she can be admired. ✓

À propos de l'auteur

Jacques Prévert est né *(born)* en 1900 à Neuilly-sur-Seine où il a grandi *(grew up).* En 1920, il s'engage *(joined)* dans l'armée. Prévert a commencé à écrire *(to write)* dans les années 30. Il est l'auteur de poèmes, mais aussi de scénarios de films dont *(of which)* les plus connus *(known)* sont *Le Crime de M. Lange* (réalisateur Jean Renoir), et *Les enfants du paradis* (Marcel Carné). Il est mort *(died)* en 1977.

~~~~~~

La terre

La terre aime le soleil
et elle tourne
pour se faire admirer[6]
et **le soleil** la trouve[7] belle
5 et il brille[8] pour elle;
et quand il est fatigué
il va **se coucher**
et **la lune** se lève.

---
[6] to be admired
[7] finds
[8] shines

"La terre" by Jacques Prévert. extrait de Aubervilliers. © Editions Gallimard.

MOTS CLÉS

la terre the earth	**la lune** the moon
le soleil the sun	**se lève** gets up / rises
se coucher to go to bed / to set	

Vocabulaire de la lecture

Mots clés

le pont *the bridge*
les messieurs *gentlemen*
les dames *ladies*
les amis *friends*
la terre *the earth*

le soleil *the sun*
la lune *the moon*
se coucher *to go to bed / to set*
se lève *gets up / rises*
danse *dances*

et *and*
aime *loves*
pour *for*
est *is*

A. Fill in each blank with the appropriate vocabulary word.

1. Les gens dansent sur le _pont_.

2. Sur le pont d'Avignon, l'on y _danse_.

3. Les beaux _messieurs_ et les belles _dames_ font comme ça.

4. La terre _aime_ le soleil.

5. Quand le soleil est fatigué, il va se _se coucher_.

6. Quand le soleil se couche, la lune _se lève_.

7. Le soleil brille _pour_ la terre.

8. Quand le soleil _est_ fatigué, il va se coucher.

B. Say whether each statement is logical or illogical.

1. Voici Thomas et Sophie. Nous sommes amis. (L) I

2. La nuit, je regarde le soleil dans le ciel *(sky)*. L (I)

3. La terre brille pour la lune. L (I)

4. À une boum, on danse. (L) I

5. J'aime ma mère. (L) I

Tu as compris?

1. Où est le pont?

Le pont est à Avignon.

2. Que font les gens sur le pont?

Les gens dansent.

3. Comment est-ce qu'ils dansent?

Ils dansent en rond.

4. Qui est-ce que la terre aime?

La terre aime le soleil.

5. Que fait le soleil quand il est fatigué?

Il va se coucher.

Connexion personnelle

How would you personify the wind if you were a poet? Brainstorm all the actions you associate with the wind.

danser
jouer
parler

le vent

chanter

Avant de lire

Comptine: C'est la poule grise
La souris

Reading Strategy

SCAN Scan the **comptine** and the poem for the names of colors, and write them in this chart.

Les Couleurs
grise noire blanche brune

What You Need To Know

La souris was written by Lucie Delarue-Mardrus, a poet and novelist who lived from 1874 to 1945. She was born in Honfleur, in Normandy. Delarue-Mardrus was a prolific writer with more than seventy works to her name, including poems, novels, biographies, plays, short stories, and memoirs.

À réfléchir...

1. What do the **comptine** and the poem have in common? **(Compare and contrast)**

They're both about animals—one is about a hen and the other is about a mouse. They're both about animals of different colors. They both rhyme.

READING TIP In many children's songs, as in poems, rhyme and rhythm are essential elements. Read the **comptine** and the poem out loud to get a good sense of both rhyme and rhythm.

READER'S SUCCESS STRATEGY Write in the words that rhyme with the following colors:

grise _l'église_

noire _l'armoire_

brune _lune_

blanche _planche_

The audio for this reading is on CD 1, Track 17.

C'est la poule grise

C'est **la poule** grise
Qui **pond** dans l'église[1];
C'est la poule noire
Qui pond dans l'armoire[2];
5 C'est la poule brune
Qui pond dans la lune;
C'est la poule blanche
Qui pond sur la planche[3].

[1] church   [2] cupboard   [3] board

MOTS CLÉS
la poule   hen   pond   lays (an egg)

The audio for this reading is on CD 1, Track 18.

À propos de l'auteur

Née en Normandie en 1874, Lucie Delarue-Mardrus était à la fois *(at the same time)* poétesse, romancière *(novelist)* et dessinatrice *(illustrator)*. Elle est surtout *(above all)* connue pour ses romans *(novels)* populaires comme *Ex-Voto,* consacré *(dedicated)* à la vie des gens de Honfleur, sa ville natale. Comme Colette, Delarue-Mardrus a célébré la naissance *(birth)* de la femme moderne du début du vingtième siècle.

~~~~~~~~~~

La souris

C'est la petite **souris** grise,
dans **sa cachette** elle est assise[4],
quand elle n'est pas dans son **trou,**
c'est qu'elle <u>galope</u> partout[5].

5 C'est la petite souris blanche
qui **ronge le pain** sur la planche,
aussitôt qu'[6]elle entend[7] **du bruit,**
dans sa maison elle s'enfuit[8].

C'est la petite souris brune
10 qui **se promène** au clair de lune[9],
si le chat **miaule** en dormant[10],
elle **se sauve** prestement[11].

[4] seated   [5] everywhere   [6] as soon as
[7] hears   [8] flees   [9] moonlight
[10] while sleeping   [11] nimbly

MOTS CLÉS

la souris mouse	**du bruit** noise
sa cachette her hiding place	**se promène** takes a walk
le trou hole	**miaule** meows
ronge gnaws	**se sauve** runs away / escapes
le pain bread	

||||À MARQUER⟩ VOCABULAIRE
In each of the boxed sections of the poem *La souris*, underline an action that seems out of character for a mouse.

CHALLENGE There is a well-known saying, "When the cat's away, the mice will play." What actions in the poem *La souris* illustrate this saying? **(Analyze)**

The grey mouse gallops and the brown mouse walks in the moonlight, but when they hear the cat meow, they run away.

Lectures supplémentaires
C'est la poule grise / La souris   63

Vocabulaire de la lecture

Mots clés

la poule *hen*
pond *lays (an egg)*
sa cachette *hiding place*
la souris *mouse*
le trou *hole*
ronge *gnaws*
le pain *bread*

du bruit *noise*
se promène *takes a walk*
miaule *meows*
se sauve *runs away / escapes*
c'est... *it's*
grise *grey*
noire *black*
blanche *white*

A. Fill in each blank with the appropriate vocabulary word.

1. La poule ___grise___ pond dans l'église.

2. La poule blanche ___pond___ sur la planche.

3. La poule ___noire___ pond dans l'armoire.

4. La souris blanche ronge ___le pain___ sur la planche.

5. La souris brune ___se promène___ au clair de lune.

6. La petite souris grise est assise dans sa ___cachette___ quand

   elle n'est pas dans son ___trou___.

7. ___C'est___ la souris blanche qui s'enfuit quand

   elle entend ___du bruit___.

B. Match the activity on the left with the appropriate animal on the right.

___b___ **1.** miaule   **a.** la souris

___c___ **2.** pond   **b.** le chat

___a___ **3.** ronge   **c.** la poule

___a___ **4.** se promène

___a___ **5.** se sauve

Tu as compris?

1. Où pond la poule noire?

Elle pond dans l'armoire.

2. Qui pond dans la lune?

La poule brune pond dans la lune.

3. Que fait la souris grise quand elle n'est pas dans son trou?

Elle galope partout.

4. Où va la souris blanche quand elle entend du bruit?

Elle va dans sa maison.

5. Comment est-ce que la souris brune se sauve si le chat miaule?

Elle se sauve prestement.

Connexion personnelle

Write your own verse about a mouse of a certain color. Use the last stanza of the poem as a model. Don't worry if it doesn't make sense; play with rhyme and rhythm.

C'est la souris bleue

Qui aime jouer aux jeux

Si le chat habite à Paris

Elle cherche tous ses amis.

Avant de lire   *Comptines: Un éléphant se balançait*
Trois poules

Reading Strategy

LOOK FOR CONTEXT CLUES At first, there might seem to be many words in the reading you can't understand. To improve your comprehension, use this strategy: read each sentence as a whole rather than translating word for word. Remember, too, to look for familiar words and see how they can help you figure out the meaning of unfamiliar ones. Fill in the box with words that you recognize.

éléphant	
alla (aller)	
allèrent (aller)	
vont	
va	
un, deux, trois (etc.)	
première, deuxième, troisième, etc.	

What You Need To Know

Nursery rhymes and **comptines** are among the first songs children hear and thus, the rhymes and songs play an important role in language learning. A common characteristic of **comptines** is repetition. Many revolve around animals and nonsensical situations. Many **comptines,** such as these two, are used to help children learn to count.

Un éléphant se balançait

Un éléphant **se balançait**
Sur **une toile d'araignée;**
Il y (trouva) tant d'agrément[1]
Qu'il <u>alla</u>[2] chercher un deuxième éléphant.

5 Deux éléphants se balançaient
Sur une toile d'araignée
Ils y (trouvèrent) tant d'agrément
Qu'ils <u>allèrent</u>[3] **chercher** un troisième éléphant.

Trois éléphants…

10 Quatre éléphants…

Cinq éléphants…

Six éléphants…

Sept éléphants…

Huit éléphants…

15 Neuf éléphants…

Dix éléphants…

---

[1] He liked it so much there (literally: he found so much pleasantness there)
[2] he went
[3] they went

MOTS CLÉS
se balancer to swing
une toile d'araignée spider web
trouver to find
chercher to look for

LECTURES SUPPLÉMENTAIRES

À réfléchir…

1. How do these **comptines** help children learn to count? (**Draw conclusions**)

In the first one, the repetition helps children learn their numbers. They learn both cardinal and ordinal numbers. The second one helps children learn the order first, second, third.

---

2. What nursery rhyme or song do you remember using to learn to count? (**Compare and contrast**)

One, Two Buckle My Shoe.

A MARQUER> GRAMMAIRE
You've learned how to conjugate the verb **aller** (to go). In the boxed sections of the first **comptine**, look for words that look like they might be forms of the verb **aller** and underline them. Find forms of **aller** in the second **comptine** and underline them. Conjugate the verb **aller** here:

je vais
tu vas
il / elle / on va
nous allons
vous allez
ils / elles vont

READING TIP The first **comptine** uses a verb form called the **passé simple**, which is sometimes called the literary past tense. The **passé simple** is no longer a spoken tense, but is often found in literature. Note the forms of **aller: alla**, and **allèrent**. Find the **passé simple** of the verb **trouver** and circle the two forms.

The audio for this reading is on CD 1, Track 20.

Trois poules

Quand trois poules s'en <u>vont</u>[3] aux **champs**

La première <u>va</u> devant.

La seconde suit[4] la première,

La troisième va derrière.

5 Quand trois poules s'en vont aux champs

La première va devant.

[3] go   [4] follows

MOTS CLÉS
    les champs .fields

Vocabulaire de la lecture

Mots clés

se balancer *to swing*
une toile d'araignée *spider web*
trouver *to find*
chercher *to look for*
les champs *fields*

aller *to go*
première *first*
deuxième *second*
troisième *third*

A. Fill in each blank with the appropriate vocabulary word.

1. Les éléphants aiment ___se balancer___ sur une ___toile d'araignée___.

2. Les poules s'en vont aux ___champs___.

3. La ___première___ va devant.

4. La ___troisième___ va derrière.

5. Il alla chercher un ___deuxième___ éléphant.

B. Write sentences using the verbs **aller, chercher, trouver.**

1. ___Je vais à l'école tous les jours.___

2. ___Nous cherchons une nouvelle maison.___

3. ___Elle ne peut pas trouver sa montre.___

Tu as compris?

1. Où est l'éléphant?

Il est sur une toile d'araignée.

2. Est-il content ou triste?

Il est content.

3. Qu'est-ce qu'il fait?

Il cherche un autre éléphant.

4. Où vont les poules?

Les poules vont aux champs.

5. Qui va devant?

La première va devant.

Connexion personnelle

Imagine your own situation for a counting rhyme that involves an animal in a silly scenario. Write your ideas here.

L'animal	Que fait-il?
un renard (fox)	Dix tortues dînent chez le renard. Une tortue tombe dans la soupe, puis, neuf tortues dînent chez le renard… etc.

Avant de lire
Comptines: Sur le fil à sécher le linge
Mère-Mouton
Mes pantoufles

Reading Strategy

WORD CHOICE Writers choose words carefully in order to express their thoughts accurately. Through careful word choice, writers can help readers visualize an image or feel a certain way. As you read *Mes pantoufles,* think about how certain words and phrases affect you as a reader. Use the chart below to record interesting words and phrases and what they convey to you.

Words and Phrases	Ideas and Feeling They Convey
en or	richness
en velours	soft, luxuriousness

What You Need To Know

Mes pantoufles is a poem written by Anne-Marie Chapouton, a writer who was born in France and who spent parts of her childhood in Tunisia, Holland, and in the United States. She received her degree in French literature from Columbia University and returned to France in 1964, where she began a long career in children's literature.

LECTURES SUPPLÉMENTAIRES

À réfléchir...

1. What is the tone of the poem *Mes pantoufles* (page 73)? **(Analyze)**

Light, carefree, magical.

2. Why does Mère Mouton threaten to knit her children's clothes from the father's wool? **(Clarify)**

Because wool is expensive this year and she has six children.

READER'S SUCCESS STRATEGY As you read the two **comptines** and the poem, highlight all the pieces of clothing that are mentioned. Sort them into the following categories.

Wear on your feet

chaussettes
pantoufles
bottes

Wear on your body / arms

manteaux
pull-over

Wear on your legs

pantalon

Sur le fil à sécher le linge

Sur **le fil à sécher le linge**
il y a un pantalon
c'est à mon cousin Gaston.

Sur le fil à sécher le linge
5 il y a un pull-over
c'est celui[1] de Philibert.

Sur le fil à sécher le linge
il y a quatre chaussettes
deux à moi, deux à Josette.

---
[1] the one (m.)

~~~~~~~~~~~

Mère-Mouton

Madame mouton **tricote**
des manteaux pour ses enfants.
Six manteaux, six paire de bottes
pour ses six petits enfants.
5 — Cette année **la laine** est chère,
dit Mère-Mouton en bêlant[2],
six cache-nez[3], six pull-overs,

---
[2] bleating   [3] nose-warmers

MOTS CLÉS
le fil à sécher le linge clothesline   **la laine** wool
tricoter to knit

READING TIP Note that **tricoterai** is the future tense of the verb **tricoter** and means *will knit*.

ça coûte beaucoup d'argent.

Et s'il fait froid cet hiver

10 je tricoterai, mes enfants,

la laine de votre père

et celle[4] de l'oncle Fernand.

[4] the one (f.)

~~~~~~~~~

The audio for this reading is on CD 1, Track 23.

À propos de l'auteur

Anne-Marie Chapouton (1939-2000) était originaire du sud de la France. Elle a consacré sa vie à la littérature pour enfants. Elle a écrit des romans et des poèmes (comme *Poèmes petits)*, mais également *(also)* des albums, en collaboration avec de nombreux illustrateurs contemporains.

Mes pantoufles

Mes pantoufles

sont en **or,**

en **velours,**

en **soie** des Indes[5].

5 Mes pantoufles

sont des **fées**

qui m'attendent

sans **bouger.**

[5] from India (Indian)

MOTS CLÉS

une pantoufle a slipper	**la soie** silk
l'or gold	**une fée** a fairy
le velours velvet	**bouger** to move, to budge

⫿⫿⫿ À MARQUER⟩ ANALYSE LITTÉRAIRE A metaphor is a comparison between two things that doesn't use "like" or "as." Underline the metaphor in the poem *Mes pantoufles.* Name the two things being compared.

slippers and fairies

CHALLENGE How are the slippers described in the poem like slippers you wore as a child? Use the Venn diagram to record your answer. Where the circles are separate, write in differences. Where they intersect, write in similarities.

Mes pantoufles

en or

en velours
je les enfile à mes pieds

en argent

Slippers from my childhood

Quand je rentre
10 de l'école
avec une
cabriole[6]
je les enfile[7]
à mes pieds.

15 Mes pantoufles
sont en or,
en velours,
en soie des Indes.
Mes pantoufles
20 sont des fées
qui **chauffent**
mes petits pieds.

---

[6] somersault   [7] I slip them on

MOTS CLÉS
chauffer to warm

Vocabulaire de la lecture

Mots clés

le fil à sécher le linge *clothesline*

tricoter *to knit*

la laine *wool*

une pantoufle *a slipper*

l'or *gold*

le velours *velvet*

la soie *silk*

une fée *a fairy*

bouger *to move, to budge*

chauffer *to warm*

un manteau *coat*

un pantalon *pants*

un pull-over *sweater*

des chaussettes *socks*

A. Match the piece of clothing on the left with the appropriate description on the right.

___c___ **1.** les pantoufles

        a. On le met pour aller dehors quand il fait froid. On le met sur les autres vêtements.

___a___ **2.** un manteau

        b. En automne, je le porte quelquefois avec un jean.

___b___ **3.** un pull-over

        c. Je les mets sur mes pieds dans la maison.

___d___ **4.** un pantalon

        d. On peut le porter pour aller à l'école. Les garçons et les filles peuvent le porter.

B. Choose three vocabulary words and write a sentence with each one.

Je vais mettre mes vêtements sur le fil à sécher le linge.

J'aime tricoter des chaussettes.

J'ai une très belle robe en soie.

Tu as compris?

1. À qui est le pull-over sur le fil à sécher le linge?

Le pull-over est à Philibert.

2. Combien de chaussettes est-ce qu'il y a sur le fil à sécher le linge?

Il y a quatre chaussettes.

3. Qu'est-ce que Madame Mouton tricote pour ses six enfants?

Elle tricote six manteaux et six paire de bottes.

4. Comment est la laine cette année?

Elle est chère.

5. Comment sont les pantoufles?

Elles sont en or, en velours, en soie des Indes.

Connexion personnelle

What ordinary everyday item might you write a poem about? Decide on a subject for your poem and write a list of words and phrases you would use to describe it in the notebook at the right.

Chaussures

petites

grandes

chères

confortables

belles

Avant de lire   *Auprès de ma blonde*

Reading Strategy

SKIM Look over the entire reading to get a sense of what it might be about. As you're skimming, look for familiar words. In this particular case, the text is a song, so look, too, for clues as to how it might be sung. Write your predictions here:

It's about a garden where birds come; it's about a blonde girl whose

husband is in Holland.

_____

_____

_____

_____

_____

What You Need To Know

Auprès de ma blonde is a French folk song that dates from the 17th century and is credited, in some instances, to André Joubert. Monsieur Joubert lived on the French island of Noirmoutiers, which was occupied by the Dutch in 1674 while France and England waged war against them. Joubert and six other men were captured and brought to Amsterdam where they were kept as hostages for two years before being released. An early version of this song appeared in 1704 under the title *Prisonnier de Hollande.* As is common for folk songs, *Auprès de ma blonde* has gone through many lyric changes. It is claimed as a traditional folk song by the Cajuns, the Québecois, and the Acadians. It was also taken up by French soldiers during World War II and sung as a peace song. **Une blonde** is slang for a *girl* or *girlfriend.*

À réfléchir...

1. How many speakers are there in the song? **(Clarify)**

There are three speakers—the person who sings the refrain, who is missing his girl; the girl who is waiting for him; and the men who ask where her husband is.

2. Based on what you've read in the song, which of the following are true? Check three. **(Summarize)**

☑ The singer's father has a beautiful garden.

☑ The dove sings for girls who aren't married.

☐ The singer isn't married.

☑ The singer's husband is in Holland.

READER'S SUCCESS STRATEGY *Auprès de ma blonde* is a folk song in the "call and response" tradition. Each successive verse starts with the last line of the previous verse and usually repeats it and introduces a new one. That way, a leader can sing the new line at the end of each verse and everyone else can join in afterwards to continue singing. To read this song like a poem, skip the repeated lines and read through to get a sense of one continuous story—or in this case—dialogue.

The audio for this reading is on CD 1, Track 24.

Auprès de ma blonde

Dans **les jardins** d'mon père
Les lilas sont fleuris[1].
Dans les jardins d'mon père
Les lilas sont fleuris.
5 Tous les oiseaux du monde
Vienn'nt y faire **leurs nids**[2].

REFRAIN
Auprès de[3] ma blonde qu'il fait bon, fait bon, fait bon
10 Auprès de ma blonde qu'il fait bon dormir!

Tous les oiseaux du monde
Vienn'nt y faire leurs nids
Tous les oiseaux du monde
Vienn'nt y faire leurs nids
15 **La caille, la tourterelle**
Et la jolie **perdrix**.

... Et ma jolie **colombe**
Qui chante jour et nuit.

[1] bloomed   [2] come make their nests there
[3] next to

MOTS CLÉS

les jardins	gardens	**la tourterelle**	turtledove
les lilas	lilacs	**la perdrix**	partridge
les nids	nests	**la colombe**	dove
la caille	quail		

Ⅲ À MARQUER ⬦ **GRAMMAIRE**
You've learned to use the **passé composé** with **avoir**. Read the boxed stanza and underline the sentence in the **passé composé**.

Qui chante pour les filles
20 Qui n'ont pas de mari.

… Pour moi ne chante guère[4]
Car j'en ai un joli[5].
… Dites-nous donc la belle
Où donc est votr'mari?

25 … Il est dans la Hollande,
Les Hollandais l'<u>ont pris.</u>

… Que donneriez-vous[6], belle
Pour avoir votr'mari?

… Je donnerais Versailles,
30 Paris et Saint-Denis.

… Les tours de Notre-Dame
Et l'clocher[7] d'mon pays.

… Et ma jolie colombe
Qui chante jour et nuit.

[4] hardly
[5] because I have a handsome one
[6] would you give
[7] church tower

READING TIP When singing in French, you usually pronounce vowels that aren't pronounced when speaking French. For example, the word **monde**, when spoken, has a silent –e at the end but would be pronounced **mon-de** when sung. Vowels not to be sung are replaced with apostrophes.

CHALLENGE Why is the girl singing about her father's garden? (**Draw conclusions**)

She is staying with her father while she waits for her husband to come home from Holland.

Vocabulaire de la lecture

Mots clés

les jardins *gardens*   **la perdrix** *partridge*

les lilas *lilacs*   **la colombe** *dove*

les nids *nests*   **le jour** *day*

la caille *quail*   **la nuit** *night*

la tourterelle *turtledove*

A. Match the vocabulary word on the left with the appropriate description on the right.

_c_ **1.** les lilas   a. C'est un oiseau qu'on peut manger.

_d_ **2.** la colombe   b. C'est une maison pour oiseaux.

_e_ **3.** un jardin   c. Ce sont des fleurs violettes qui
                                   sentent *(smell)* bonnes.

_a_ **4.** la caille   d. C'est un oiseau blanc, utilisé comme
                                   symbole pour la paix.

_b_ **5.** un nid   e. C'est un endroit avec beaucoup de fleurs.

B. Write one sentence for each of the remaining vocabulary words.

La tourterelle est grise.

La perdrix ne chante pas.

Je vais passer trois jours à la montagne.

Bonne nuit, maman!

Tu as compris?

1. À qui est le jardin?

C'est le jardin du père de la chanteuse / de la femme.

2. Quel fleur est-ce qu'il y a dans le jardin?

Il y a les lilas.

3. Que fait tous les oiseaux là-bas?

Ils y font leur nids.

4. Pourqui est-ce que la colombe chante?

La colombe chante pour les filles qui n'ont pas de mari.

5. Où est le mari de la chanteuse? Pourquoi?

Il est dans la Hollande. Les Hollandais l'ont pris.

Connexion personnelle

How might you describe your backyard or garden? What words or phrases would you choose to describe what happens there? Make a list here.

Mon jardin

Il y a de jolies fleurs blanches.

Beaucoup d'oiseaux viennent se baigner.

Les papillons volent.

Avant de lire
Comptines: En allant chercher mon pain
Monsieur de Saint-Laurent
Les bonbons

Reading Strategy

CONNECT TO YOUR OWN LIFE You can connect the subject of a reading to your own life. As you read these **comptines**, think about foods that you like to eat. Compare the foods mentioned as preferences in *Les bonbons* and write your own list of favorite foods.

Les Bonbons	My Preferences
les bonbons la cannelle les gâteaux le chocolat	le chocolat les hamburgers le poulet le fromage

What You Need To Know

The French are famous for the high value they place on food. **Gourmandise** is a French term that appears to have several meanings. According to Jean Anthelme Brillat-Savarin, who wrote *The Physiology of Taste* in 1826, **gourmandise** is the "passionate preference, well-determined and satisfied, for objects which flatter our taste" and not, as some dictionaries seemed to suggest, a "confusion of gluttony and voracity." Still, today **gourmandise** can mean either of the following:
1) a taste and relish for good food;
2) to overeat or eat immodestly, make a pig of oneself.

The audio for these readings is on CD 1, Tracks 25–26.

En allant chercher mon pain

En allant chercher mon pain
Je rencontre trois lapins,
<u>Je les mets</u> dans mon panier[1],
Ils me boivent tout mon lait;
5 <u>Je les mets</u> dans mon placard[2],
Ils me mangent tout mon **lard;**
<u>Je les mets</u> au coin du feu[3],
Ils me font trois petits oeufs,
    Bleu, blanc, rouge.

~~~~~~~~~~

Monsieur de Saint-Laurent

Monsieur de Saint-Laurent,
La canne en argent[4],
Le bouton doré[5],
Qu'avez-vous mangé?
5 — J'ai mangé un oeuf,
La moitié[6] d'un **boeuf,**
Quatre-vingts moutons,
Autant de[7] **chapons;**
J'ai bu la rivière,
10 Et j'ai encore faim!
— Monsieur de Saint-Laurent,
Vous êtes un gourmand.

---

[1] basket   [2] closet   [3] in a corner of the hearth
[4] silver cane   [5] golden button   [6] half   [7] as many

MOTS CLÉS
  le lard bacon
  le boeuf beef
                           le chapon capon (a type
                                 of chicken)

À réfléchir...

1. Number the phrases to show the order in which the rabbits in the first **comptine** do the following things. **(Chronological order)**

   __3__   lay three eggs

   __1__   drink milk

   __2__   eat the bacon

2. According to the second **comptine,** what is the definition of a **gourmand?** **(Draw conclusions)**

Someone who eats a lot of food; a glutton.

▥▐ À MARQUER ▷ GRAMMAIRE
In this unit, you've learned to use direct object pronouns. In the first **comptine,** underline the phrases with direct object pronouns.

READING TIP These **comptines** contain a lot of familiar food vocabulary. Some new words you can figure out, such as **les vermicelles** (which is a cognate). Although it doesn't mean the exact same thing as the English word, **le lard** means *bacon,* which is definitely related.

Lectures supplémentaires
En allant chercher mon pain /
Monsieur de Saint-Laurent /
Les bonbons   **83**

The audio for this reading is on CD 1, Track 27.

Les bonbons

J'aime mieux les bonbons
que le **gigot de mouton,**
j'aime mieux la cannelle[8]
que les vermicelles,
5 j'aime mieux les gâteaux
que la **soupe aux poireaux.**
J'ai des confitures
sur toute la figure
et du chocolat
10 du haut jusqu'en bas[9].
Moustache de chat
filet de foie gras.

---

[8] cinnamon   [9] from top to bottom

Le petit déjeuner
le lard
les oeufs
la confiture

Le dîner
le mouton / le gigot de mouton
la soupe aux poireaux

Le dessert
les gâteaux
le chocolat
les bonbons

CHALLENGE Who do you
think is the speaker of the
comptine *Les bonbons* and
why? **(Draw conclusions)**

Small child — because he or
she likes candy and chocolate
instead of other foods that are
better for you.

MOTS CLÉS
  le gigot de mouton leg of lamb   **la soupe aux poireaux** leek soup

Vocabulaire de la lecture

Mots clés

le lard *bacon*
le boeuf *beef*
le chapon *capon (a type of chicken)*
le gigot de mouton *leg of lamb*
la soupe aux poireaux *leek soup*

le pain *bread*
le lait *milk*
les oeufs *eggs*
le gâteau *cake*
la confiture *jam*

A. Match the item of food on the left with the appropriate description on the right.

_d_ **1.** le chapon

_e_ **2.** les oeufs

_b_ **3.** le lait

_c_ **4.** le pain

_a_ **5.** la soupe aux poireaux

a. On la mange avec une cuillière.

b. On le boit.

c. On le mange souvent le matin avec du beurre.

d. C'est un oiseau qu'on peut manger.

e. C'est un produit qui vient des poules.

B. Fill in each blank with an appropriate vocabulary word.

1. Le samedi matin, j'aime manger des oeufs avec du _lard_.

2. Demain, c'est mon anniversaire. On va me faire un _gâteau_.

3. Est-ce que tu vas mettre de la _confiture_ sur ton pain?

4. Au printemps, on mange souvent le _gigot de mouton_.

5. Anne est végétarienne. Elle ne mange pas de _boeuf_.

Tu as compris?

1. Qu'est-ce que les lapins ont bu?

Ils ont bu tout le lait.

2. Qu'est-ce que les lapins ont mangé?

Ils ont mangé tout le lard.

3. Combien de moutons est-ce que Monsieur de Saint-Laurent a mangé?

Il a mangé quatre-vingts moutons.

4. Qu'est-ce qu'il a bu?

Il a bu la rivière.

Connexion personnelle

Make a list of foods that you like. List them on the chart and write a couple of reasons why you like each one.

La Nourriture	Les Raisons
les frites	J'aime les choses salées; j'aime les pommes de terre.

Academic and
Informational Reading

Academic and Informational Reading

In this section you'll find strategies to help you read all kinds of informational materials. The examples here range from magazines you read for fun to textbooks to bus schedules. Applying these simple and effective techniques will help you be a successful reader of the many texts you encounter every day.

Reading a Magazine Article

A magazine article is designed to catch and hold your interest. You will get the most from your reading if you recognize the special features of a magazine page and learn how to use them. Look at the sample magazine article as you read each strategy below.

A Read the **title** to get an idea of what the article is about. Scan any other **headings** to see how information in the article is organized.

B As you read, notice any **quotations.** Who is quoted? Is the person a reliable source on the subject?

C Notice information set in special type, such as **italics** or **boldface.** For example, look at the quotation in the article that is set in italic type.

D Study **visuals,** such as charts, graphs, pictures, maps, and bulleted lists. Visuals add important information and bring the topic to life.

MARK IT UP Read the magazine article on the next page. Use the tips above to help you answer the following questions.

1. What is the topic of this article? _the Tour de France bicycle race_
   _____

2. Underline the distance covered during the modern Tour de France.

3. Do you think the speaker of the quotation set off in italic type is a reliable source of information on the Tour de France? Why or why not?
   Yes, since he's the top official of the Tour

4. Have women ever participated in this elite bicycle race? If so, when?
   Yes, between 1984 and 1989

5. Circle the chart that gives interesting facts about the Tour de France.

CYCLING'S SUPREME CHALLENGE—THE TOUR DE FRANCE

A

Everyone loves jumping on a bike and pedaling around for enjoyment and exercise. Increasing numbers of people even rely on cycling as their major means of transportation. But for those elite athletes whose lives revolve around cycling, there are just three words—Tour de France.

The idea for the Tour de France, the world's ultimate bicycle race, was hatched at a business lunch in Paris just over a century ago. It was based on a six-day track race, but with the riders wending their way through the country instead of going in circles. The first race, held in 1903, totaled 2,428 km.

Today, the race covers 3,427 km (2,100 miles) in 20 stages, or separate races, that begin and end in the same day. Each stage has a winner, and the rider with the lowest total time at the end of the three weeks becomes the overall champion. The cyclists race in

teams, with each team often working together to ensure that one of its members wins. The Tour is restricted to men, although races for women were held from 1984 to 1989.

C

"The Tour de France," says current Tour chief Jean-Marie Leblanc, "is an uncommon human adventure . . . ."

Part of what makes the race such an unusual and exciting event is the fact that the fans don't have to go to it—it comes to them. People along the route can reach out and touch the cyclists, and have been known to hand racers a water bottle or even offer a helpful push.

France has given the world not only one of its most mouth-watering cuisines, but also the most athletically challenging way to work off all those calories. In the words of three-time Tour winner, American Greg LeMond, "You couldn't have this race in any other country." B

D

Number of chains worn out by a single rider	3
Youngest winner	20	Oldest winner	36
Average calories consumed by a rider per day	5,900
Total calories burned by a rider	123,900
Total number of pedal strokes	324,000 (at 60 rpm)
Winner's prize	€400,000

Add It Up—Tour Tidbits

Reading a Textbook

The first page of a textbook lesson introduces you to a particular topic. The page also provides important information that will guide you through the rest of the lesson. Look at the sample textbook page as you read each strategy below.

A Preview the **title** and other **headings** to find out the lesson's main topic and related subtopics.

B Read the **key ideas** or **objectives** at the top of the page. Keep these in mind as you read. They will help you set a purpose for your reading.

C Look for a list of terms or **vocabulary words** at the start of each lesson. These words will be identified and defined throughout the lesson.

D Study **visuals** such as photographs and illustrations. Read the **captions.** Visuals can add information and interest to the topic.

MARK IT UP Read the sample textbook page. Then use the strategies above to help you answer the following questions.

1. What is the topic of this lesson? This lesson is about waves and erosion.

_____

2. Circle the key idea of the lesson.

3. Draw a box around the vocabulary words that will be defined in the lesson.

4. Put a star next to the visual that shows the structure of a sea arch.

5. Using a graphic organizer can help you take notes on the textbook material you learn. Complete the chart using information on shoreline features from the lesson.

| Waves strike headlands. | → | Notch is formed. | → | Notch deepens to become sea cave. | → | Waves cut through walls of sea cave to form sea arch. | → | Roof of sea arch falls in, leaving sea stack. |

A Shoreline Features

Ocean waves change the shape of a shoreline by eroding rock materials and by depositing sediments.

Waves and Erosion

Breaking storm waves may strike rock cliffs with a force of thousands of kilograms per square meter. Such breakers easily remove large masses of loose sand and clay. Air and water driven into cracks and fissures may split bedrock apart. Sand and pebbles carried by the water abrade the bedrock. Waves pound loose rock and boulders into pebbles and sand. In addition, seawater dissolves minerals from rocks such as limestone.

When waves strike the headlands of a deep-water shoreline, they may cut away the rock up to the high-tide level, forming a notch. If the materials overhanging the notch collapse, a sea cliff results.

Cliffs made of soft materials such as soil and sand wear away very quickly. For example, waves washing up on Cape Cod in Massachusetts are carrying away materials from sand cliffs there so rapidly that the cliffs are receding at a rate of about one meter every year.

In cliffs made of harder rock materials, a notch may deepen until it becomes a sea cave. Waves may cut through the walls of sea caves to form sea arches. Arches may also form when waves cut through vertical cracks in narrow headlands. If the roof of a sea arch falls in, what remains is a tall, narrow rock island called a sea stack.

Sea caves, sea arches, and sea stacks can be seen on the coasts of California, Oregon, Washington, and Maine, on the Gaspé Peninsula of Canada, and in many parts of the Mediterranean Sea.

16.3

B **KEY IDEA**

Waves erode shorelines and deposit sediments in characteristic formations.

C **KEY VOCABULARY**
- beach
- sandbar
- fjord

BAJA PENINSULA Ocean waves have formed this sea stack and sea arch in Mexico.

D

Sea stack

Sea arch

349

Reading a Table

Tables give a lot of information in an organized way. These tips can help you read a table quickly and accurately. Look at the example as you read each strategy in this list.

A Look at the **title** to find out the content of the table.

B Read the **introduction** to get a general overview of the information included in the table.

C Examine the **heading** of each row and column. To find specific information, locate the place where a row and column intersect.

B Water temperatures vary widely along the coasts of North America. This table shows the temperature of the water in March at seven beaches.

A Average March Water Temperature at Eight Beaches (°F)

C

Location	Temperature	Location	Temperature
Newport, RI	37	Seattle, WA	46
Ocean City, MD	42	Honolulu, HI	76
Freeport, TX	62	Juneau, AK	37
Oceanside, CA	58		

MARK IT UP Answer the following questions using the table of March water temperatures.

1. Which two beaches have the same water temperature? Circle the answers in the table.

2. What units are used to measure the water temperatures?

degrees Fahrenheit
_____

3. If you were planning a swimming vacation in March, what beach might you consider visiting?

Honolulu, HI
_____

Reading a Map

To read a map correctly, you have to identify and understand its elements. Look at the example below as you read each strategy in this list.

A Read the **title** to find out what the map shows.

B Study the **legend,** or **key,** to find out what symbols and colors are used on the map and what they stand for.

C Look at **geographic labels** to understand specific places on the map.

D Look at the **scale** to understand how distances on the map relate to actual distances.

E Locate the **compass rose,** or **pointer,** to determine direction.

A English-French Bilingualism in 2001

B Percentage of population who speak English and French
- 50.0–70.3
- 35.0–49.9
- 20.0–34.9
- 10.0–19.9
- 5.0–9.9
- 0–4.9

170°W 160°W

C ARCTIC OCEAN

Hudson Bay

C A N A D A

D 0 250 500 miles
0 250 500 kilometers

E N

70°W

MARK IT UP Use the map to answer the following questions.

1. What does this map show? _the distribution of bilingual speakers in_
   Canada in 2001

2. In how many separate areas of Canada is more than half the population bilingual?
   two

3. Where in Canada do most of the people who speak only English live?
   In the north central part of the country

4. Draw a straight line between the most easterly and most westerly points in Canada. About how many miles across is the country?
   about 3,300 miles

Reading a Diagram

Diagrams combine pictures with a few words to provide
a lot of information. Look at the example on the opposite
page as you read each of the following strategies.

A Look at the **title** to get an idea of what the diagram is
about.

B Study the **images** closely to understand each part of the
diagram.

C Look at the **captions** and the **labels** for more information.

||MARK IT UP⟩ Study the diagram, then answer the following questions using
the strategies above.

1. What does this diagram illustrate? _____

   the structure of composite volcanoes and cinder cones

   _____

2. What is one example of a composite volcano? _____

   Mount Shasta in California

   _____

3. What is one difference between cinder cones and composite volcanoes?

   Cinder cones tend to be smaller than composite volcanoes and to form in groups.

   _____

4. Circle the name of the layer of the earth that lies under the continental crust.

5. Draw a box around the part of the diagram that shows the internal structure
   of a composite volcano.

A Volcanic Landforms

The shape and structure of a volcano are determined by the nature of its eruptions and the materials it ejects. A cinder cone, perhaps the simplest form of volcano, forms when molten lava is thrown into the air from a vent. Cinder cones, which tend to be smaller than other types of volcanoes, typically form in groups and on the sides of larger volcanoes. Composite volcanoes develop when layers of materials from successive eruptions accumulate around a vent. The diagram shows the structure of these two types of volcanoes.

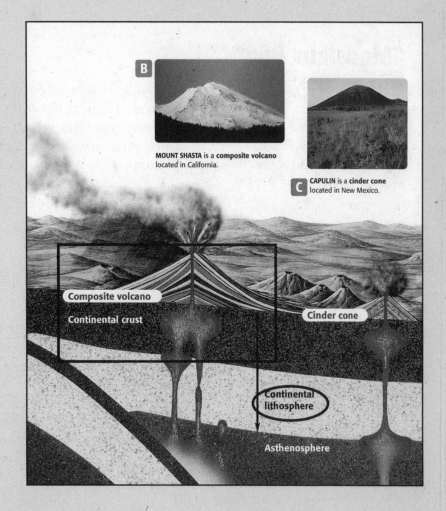

B

MOUNT SHASTA is a **composite volcano** located in California.

C CAPULIN is a **cinder cone** located in New Mexico.

Composite volcano

Continental crust

Cinder cone

Continental lithosphere

Asthenosphere

The *main idea* in a paragraph is its most important point. *Details* in the paragraph support the main idea. Identifying the main idea will help you focus on the main message the writer wants to communicate. Use the following strategies to help you identify a paragraph's main idea and supporting details.

- Look for the **main idea,** which is often the first sentence in a paragraph.

- Use the main idea to help you **summarize** the point of the paragraph.

- Identify specific **details,** including facts and examples, that support the main idea.

"Monsieur Rap"

Main idea

The French king of rap music is a rhythmic sensation called MC Solaar. Born in Senegal to parents from Chad and raised in France, he writes songs that continue to bridge cultural barriers. They weave clever French word play into American rap rhythms to communicate a global message of hope. Solaar has put his ideals into action by singing to support the release of political prisoners around the world.

Details —

MARK IT UP Read the following paragraph. Circle the main idea. Then underline the details that support the main idea.

MC Solaar has truly become an international sensation. In 1991, he teamed up with the American rap group De la Soul at a concert in Paris. In 1992, he toured extensively through Russia and Poland and gave performances in a dozen West African countries. Three years later, after being named Best Male Singer of the Year at the 10th French "Victoires de la Musique" awards, he traveled and performed throughout France and Europe. His albums remain best-sellers in more than 20 countries.

Problem and Solution

Does the proposed solution to a problem make sense? In order to decide, you need to look at each part of the text. Use the following strategies to read the text below.

- Look at the beginning or middle of a paragraph to find the **statement of the problem.**
- Find **details** that explain the problem and tell why it is important.
- Look for the **proposed solution.**
- Identify the **supporting details** for the proposed solution.
- Think about whether the solution is a good one.

Lunchroom Language Tables Can Beef Up Students' Skills

by Tara Blum

Statement of problem

Teachers, parents, administrators, and school board members are concerned that foreign language students are not getting enough practice actually using the language in conversation.

Details about the problem

In their foreign language classes, students read dialogs from their textbooks and respond to questions, but rarely get a chance to just communicate their thoughts.

Proposed solution

One way to address this problem would be to establish language tables in the lunchroom. Students taking a specific language would eat their lunch at a designated table one day a week. The only rule would be that they must speak no English, just the foreign language.

Details about the solution

This plan has several advantages. First, it doesn't require any additional equipment or materials. Second, it wouldn't take time away from other classes or activities. Language students have to eat lunch just like everyone else. Finally, it would be a lot of fun.

Language tables would let students supplement their language skills while nourishing their bodies. And that's a recipe for success!

⫸ **MARK IT UP** ⫸ Use the text and strategies above to answer these questions.

1. Underline the proposed solution.

2. Circle at least one reason that supports this solution.
Answers will vary. A sample answer has been circled.

3. Explain why you think this is or is not a good solution to the problem.

This is a good solution because it would get students using foreign language without a

teacher present in a fun setting. / This is not a good solution because kids would resent

not eating with their friends and wouldn't follow the no-English rule.

Sequence

Sequence is the order in which events happen. Whether you read a story or a social studies lesson, it is important for you to understand *when* things happen in relation to one another. The tips below can help you identify sequence in any type of text.

- Look for the **main steps** or **events** in the sequence.
- Look for **words and phrases that signal time**, such as *in ancient times* and *today*.
- Look for **words and phrases that signal order**, such as *first, after,* and *next*.

MARK IT UP > Read the passage about making cheese on the next page. Then use the information from the article and the tips above to answer the questions.

1. Underline two words or phrases that signal time.
   Answers will vary. Possible answers are underlined.

2. Circle two words or phrases that signal order.
   Answers will vary. Possible answers are circled.

3. A flowchart can help you identify and understand a sequence of events. Use the information from the passage to complete this flowchart.

Cheese is made from milk. The first step is ___acidification___ .

↓

The milk seperates into curds and whey. Then ___coagulation___ turns milk into curds and whey.

↓

The curds are heated and cut, and salt is added. The curds ___are shaped into___ cheeses.

↓

The cheese is left to age. Finally the cheese ___ripens___ .

Say Cheese

You've sliced it, diced it, melted it, spiced it—eaten it spread on crackers, over vegetables, with fruit, or by itself. You're friends with American and Swiss, and have maybe tried one of the more than 400 varieties of cheese that the French produce with pride and call *fromage*. But have you ever thought about how cheese is made?

All cheese starts with milk—from cows, goats, sheep, or other animals. In fact, if the mozzarella that tops your pizza is authentic, it came from buffaloes. According to one story, an Arab nomad accidentally made the first cheese in ancient times when the hot sun, his horse's motion, and a chemical in a saddlebag of milk turned the liquid into white lumps.

The basic cheese-making principle this Arab discovered is that milk naturally curdles, or separates into solid curds and liquid whey. The first step in helping this process along involves making the milk more acidic. This is done by adding bacteria that change the sugar in milk into lactic acid in the process of acidification.

After acidification, coagulation—turning milk into curds and whey—begins. A chemical enzyme helps the curds become solid. This enzyme occurs in rennet, which comes from the lining of calves' stomachs. Today, scientists artificially create this enzyme using yeast cells.

The curds are then heated and cut to help release any liquid that remains. Next salt is added to improve the taste and kill unwanted bacteria, and the curds are shaped in a cheese press.

Finally the remaining bacteria help the cheese ripen, or age. At this stage, other bacteria, like the ones that produce penicillin, may be added to help create the blue veins in bleu cheese and the white coating on Brie and Camembert. This process can take from days to decades, depending on the type of cheese being made.

So, next time you want a snack, just think about this process, smile, and say "cheese"!

Cause and Effect

A *cause* is an event that brings about another event. An *effect* is something that happens as a result of the first event. Identifying causes and effects helps you understand how events are related. Use the tips below to find causes and effects in any kind of reading.

- Look for an action or event that answers the question, "What happened?" This is the **effect.**

- Look for an action or event that answers the question, "Why did this happen?" This is the **cause.**

- Look for words or phrases that **signal** causes and effects, such as *because, as a result, therefore, consequently,* and *since.*

MARK IT UP > Read the cause-and-effect passage on the next page. Notice that the first cause and effect are labeled. Then use the strategies above to help you answer the following questions.

1. Circle words in the passage that signal causes and effects. The first one has been done for you.

2. Some causes may have more than one effect. What are two effects of the mosquito's saliva on the body of the victim?

   It prevents blood from clotting and triggers an allergic reaction.
   _____

   _____

3. Complete the following diagram showing the cause and effects of mosquito bites.

   Effect: Punctures victim's skin

   Cause: Female mosquito needs blood to nourish her eggs.

   Effect: Injects saliva and sucks victim's blood.

   Effect: Victim has allergic reaction to saliva and develops itchy bump.

Bzz! Slap!

Cause

If you spend any time outdoors in the summer, at some point you will probably find yourself covered with mosquito bites.

Mosquitoes can transmit serious diseases such as yellow fever, encephalitis, and malaria. Usually, though, mosquito bites just (cause) people to develop raised, red bumps that itch like crazy.

Signal
Word
Effect

This is what happens. Female mosquitoes need blood to nourish the eggs developing in their bodies. (Consequently,) they zero in on living things whose blood they can suck. Once they find a likely victim, the attack begins.

This attack is not really a bite, since a mosquito isn't able to open her jaws. Instead, she punctures the victim's skin with sharp stylets inside her mouth. The mosquito's saliva then flows into these puncture wounds. (Because) the saliva keeps the victim's blood from clotting, the mosquito can drink her fill. This can sometimes amount to 150 percent of the mosquito's weight.

Meanwhile, the mosquito's saliva sets off an allergic reaction in the victim. (As a result) the person develops the itchy swelling we call a mosquito bite. Ironically, if the

mosquito finishes eating before the victim slaps or drives her off, there will be less saliva left in the skin. (Therefore,) the allergic reaction and itching will not be so severe.

Here are some steps you can take to help prevent mosquito bites or lessen their effect if you do get bitten.

- Don't go out at prime mosquito time—from dusk to dawn.
- Use insect repellent at all times.
- If you do get bitten, DON'T SCRATCH. Scratching just increases the allergic reaction.

Comparison and Contrast

Comparing two things means showing how they are the same. *Contrasting* two things means showing how they are different. Comparisons and contrasts are important because they show how things or ideas are related. Use these tips to help you understand comparison and contrast in reading assignments such as the article on the opposite page.

- Look for **direct statements** of **comparison and contrast.** "These things are similar because…" or "One major difference is…"

- Pay attention to **words and phrases that signal comparisons**, such as *also, both, in addition to,* and *in the same way.*

- Notice **words and phrases that signal contrasts**. Some of these are *however, on the other hand, but,* and *in contrast.*

 Read the article on the next page. Then use the information from the article and the tips above to answer the questions.

1. Circle the words and phrases that signal comparisons. A sample has been done for you.

2. Underline the words and phrases that signal contrast. Notice the completed example.

3. A Venn diagram shows how two subjects are similar and how they are different. Complete this diagram, which uses information from the essay to compare and contrast greetings in France and America. Add one or more similarity to the center of the diagram and one or more difference to each outer circle.

French greetings

Use of pronouns shows relationship between people

non-family shake hands hello and goodbye, family members kiss morning and evening, girls exchange une bise, teen boys shake hands and may give une bise to girlfriends

Both

way of saying hello and goodbye

greeting determined by relationship, girls more affectionate than boys

American greetings

family members kiss good night

teen girls may hug, everyone addressed as you, fathers often shake hands with sons, informal greetings among non-family, boys may give pats or punches

Greetings Across the Atlantic

No matter where you were born and live, you're becoming more and more a citizen of a global community. Nevertheless, differences between cultures still—and probably always will—exist. One important characteristic of a culture is how people say hello and goodbye to each other. Here's how it's done in America and a close neighbor across the ocean, France.

Comparison

In (both) cultures, the relationship between people determines how they greet one another. The French language includes a way of showing this relationship. In formal situations, people address each other using the pronoun *vous*. Informal and close relationships are marked by the use of *tu*. In America, the language offers no such help, however, since everyone is just addressed as *you*.

Contrast

American family members often kiss each other goodnight, although fathers may choose instead to shake hands with their teenage sons. To people outside the family, Americans usually offer informal greetings—a smile, a nod of the head, or a simple, "Hi, how are you?" Among teens, girlfriends also may exchange hugs, and boys, pats or punches on the arm or back.

(Like) Americans, the French greet family members with kisses, but not only when going to bed. They (also) kiss hello in the morning and when seeing each other again during the day. (In addition,) fathers are not as reluctant as American men to kiss their sons.

On the other hand, French people are more formal than Americans when greeting non-family-members. They shake hands and offer a formal acknowledgement with the person's title both when they meet and part. French boys (also) greet one another with handshakes, though they often give a girlfriend *une bise*, or several kisses on the cheeks. Teenage girls usually exchange *une bise* with both girlfriends and boyfriends.

So now you know how to give warmest greetings—in your own special way—on either side of the Atlantic!

Persuasion

To be persuasive, an opinion should be backed up with reasons and facts. After you carefully read an opinion and the reasons and facts that support it, you will be able to decide if the opinion makes sense. As you read these tips, look at the sample persuasive essay on the next page.

- Look for words or phrases that **signal an opinion**, such as *I believe, I think,* and *in my opinion.*

- Identify reasons, facts, or expert opinions that **support** the position.

- Ask yourself if the opinion and the reasons that back it up **make sense.**

- Look for **errors in reasoning,** such as overgeneralizations, that may affect the presentation of the opinion.

 MARK IT UP Read the persuasive essay on the following page. Then use the strategies above to help you answer the following questions.

1. Underline any words or phrases that signal the writer's opinion.

2. Circle any words or phrases that signal the opinion of persons other than the writer.

3. The writer presents both sides of this debate. List the points supporting both sides in the chart below. One reason has been provided for you.

For swimming pool	Against swimming pool
1. The school has a responsibility to teach swimming.	1. Students can take swimming lessons at the health club.
2. Most students don't have money or time to take private swimming lessons.	2. Money must be used to repair school building.
3. Students' education is more important than building repairs.	
4. Swimming is an excellent form of exercise.	

Our School Needs to Get in the Swim *by Eric Legrand*

This school needs a swimming pool. Swimming is an important life skill and I believe it is the responsibility of the school to provide this essential part of students' education.

The school's mission is to educate the whole person—mind and body—and to prepare students to be productive citizens. In addition to our academic subjects, we are taught how to eat right, budget our money, and drive a car. But we don't learn the water safety skills that could someday save our lives.

The community and school board obviously don't feel the way I do, however. They repeatedly have refused to fund the building of a pool. In the opinion of one board member, "Students can take swimming lessons at the local health club." Other school officials think that the school has more important needs—repairing the sagging gym floor and installing new lockers, for example.

In my opinion, these reasons are not valid. First, most students cannot afford lessons at the health club. Even those who have the money don't have the time. They're busy with homework and other activities during the school year and have to work or go to summer school during vacation.

I agree that the gym floor should be replaced and wouldn't mind having a new locker. But I believe that the educational needs of the students should come first. Swimming is one of the best forms of exercise there is. Even if knowing how to swim never saves your life, it can improve its quality. Isn't that what an education is all about?

Social Studies

Social studies class becomes easier when you understand how your textbook's words, pictures, and maps work together to give you information. Following these tips can make you a better reader of social studies lessons. As you read the tips, look at the sample lesson on the right-hand page.

A Read the **title** of the lesson and other **headings** to find out what the lesson is about. Smaller headings may introduce subtopics that are related to the main topic.

B Read the **main ideas** or **objectives** listed on the first page of the lesson. These items summarize the lesson and help set a purpose for your reading.

C Look at the **vocabulary terms** listed on the lesson's first page. These terms will be boldfaced or underlined where they appear in the text.

D Notice **how information is organized.** In social studies lessons, ideas are often presented using sequence, cause and effect, comparison and contrast, and main idea and supporting details.

E Carefully examine **visual features** such as photographs, boxed text, maps, charts, bulleted lists, time lines, diagrams, and information in the margins. Think about how the visuals and the text are related.

MARK IT UP Carefully read the textbook page at right. Use the information from the text and from the tips above to answer the questions.

1. What is the topic of this lesson? <u>the fight of people in Latin America against colonial rule</u>

2. The ideas in the subsection "The Fight for Freedom" are presented in chronological sequence. Which other type of organization is used—comparison and contrast or main idea and supporting details?

   <u>main idea and supporting details</u>

3. Why did the French put Toussaint L'Ouverture in prison?

   <u>They thought he was planning to rise up against them a second time.</u>

4. Underline the sentence that describes who carried on Toussaint's work after he died.

5. Which important idea does the photograph of the statue illustrate?

   <u>the importance of freedom to enslaved African people in the French colony of Saint-Domingue</u>

---

1 Latin American Peoples Win Independence

TERMS & NAMES C
- *peninsulares*
- creoles
- mulattos
- Simón Bolívar
- José de San Martín
- Miguel Hidalgo
- José Morelos

MAIN IDEA	WHY IT MATTERS NOW
Spurred by discontent and Enlightenment ideas, peoples in Latin America fought colonial rule.	Sixteen of today's Latin American nations gained their independence at this time.

SETTING THE STAGE By the late 1700s, the Americas, already troubled by Enlightenment ideas, were electrified by the news of the French Revolution. The French ideals of liberty, equality, and fraternity inspired many Latin Americans to rise up against their French, Spanish, and Portuguese masters.

Revolution in Haiti

The French colony called Saint Domingue was the first Latin American territory to free itself from European rule. Saint Domingue, now known as Haiti, occupied the western third of the island of Hispaniola in the Caribbean Sea.

Background
About 35,000 Europeans stood at the top of the social ladder in Haiti in the late 1700s. They were mainly French.

Nearly 500,000 enslaved Africans—the vast majority of Saint Domingue's population—lived at the bottom of the social system. Most slaves worked on plantations, and they outnumbered their masters dramatically. White masters thus used brutal methods to terrorize slaves and keep them powerless.

The Fight for Freedom The slaves soon showed that, in fact, they were not powerless. In August 1791, an African priest named Boukman raised a call for revolution. Within a few days, 100,000 slaves rose in revolt. A leader soon emerged, Toussaint L'Ouverture (too-SAN loo-vair-TOOR), an ex-slave. Toussaint was untrained in the military and in diplomacy. Even so, he rose to become a skilled general and diplomat. It is said that he got the name L'Ouverture ("opening" in French) because he was so skilled at finding openings in the enemy lines. By 1801, Toussaint had moved into Spanish Santo Domingo (the eastern two-thirds of Hispaniola). He took control of the territory and freed the slaves.

In January 1802, 16,000 French troops landed in Saint Domingue to depose Toussaint. In May, Toussaint agreed to halt the revolution if the French would end slavery. Despite the agreement, the French soon accused him of planning another uprising. They seized him and sent him to a prison in the French Alps. In that cold mountain jail, he died 10 months later, in April 1803.

Background
By 1600, almost the entire Arawak population had disappeared because of European conquest, warfare, disease, or slavery.

Haiti's Independence Toussaint's general, Jean-Jacques Dessalines (zhahn-ZHAHK day-sah-LEEN), took up the fight for freedom where Toussaint had left off. On January 1, 1804, General Dessalines declared the colony an independent country. It was the first black colony to free itself from European control. He called the country Haiti, which meant "mountainous land" in the language of the native Arawak inhabitants of the island.

E

This statue, called *The Unknown Maroon of Saint Domingue*, stands in front of Haiti's National Palace. *Maroon* was a name for runaway slaves. Using a shell as a trumpet, the maroon is sounding the call to freedom.

Science

Reading a science textbook becomes easier when you understand how the explanations, drawings, and special terms work together. Use the strategies below to help you better understand your science textbook. Look at the examples on the opposite page as you read each strategy in this list.

A Preview the **title** and any **headings** to see what scientific concepts you will learn about.

B Read the **key ideas** or **objectives.** These items summarize the lesson and help set a purpose for your reading.

C Read the list of **vocabulary terms** that will be introduced and defined in the lesson.

D Notice the **boldfaced** and **italicized** terms in the text. Look for the definitions of these terms.

E Carefully examine any **pictures** or **diagrams.** Read the **captions** to see how the graphics help to illustrate the text.

 Use the strategies above and the science lesson on the next page to answer these questions.

1. Underline the title of the lesson.

2. Circle the list of vocabulary words that will appear in the lesson.

3. Draw a box around one boldfaced term in the lesson.

4. Examine the graph and read the text directly above it. What idea does the graph illustrate?

   The graph illustrates how the elevation of the snow line changes in relation to a

   given latitude.

5. At what latitude is the elevation of the snow line lowest?

   at the North Pole

15.1

B KEY IDEAS

Glaciers are huge ice masses that move under the influence of gravity.

Glaciers form from compacted and recrystallized snow.

C KEY VOCABULARY

- glacier
- snow line
- firn
- valley glacier
- continental glacier
- ice cap

A ## What Is a Glacier?

About 75 percent of Earth's fresh water is frozen in glaciers. A **glacier** is a large mass of compacted snow and ice that moves under the force of gravity. A glacier changes Earth's surface as it erodes geological features in one place and then redeposits the material elsewhere thus altering the landscape.

Where Glaciers Form

Glaciers form in areas that are always covered by snow. In such areas, more snow falls than melts each year; as a result layers of snow build up from previous years. Climates cold enough to cause such conditions may be found in any part of the world. Air temperatures drop as you climb high above sea level and as you travel farther from the equator.

Even in equatorial areas, however, a layer of permanent snow may exist on high mountains at high elevation. Farther from the equator, the elevation need not be so high for a layer of permanent snow to exist. In the polar areas, permanent snow may be found even at sea level. The lowest elevation at which the layer of permanent snow occurs in summer is called **D** the **snow line.** If a mountain is completely covered with snow in winter but without snow in summer, it has no snow line.

In general, the snow line occurs at lower and lower elevations as the latitudes approach the poles. The snow line also changes according to total yearly snowfall and the amount of solar exposure. Thus, the elevation of the snow line is not the same for all places at a given latitude.

VISUALIZATIONS
CLASSZONE.COM

Examine seasonal migration of snow cover.
Keycode: ES1501

E

Snow Line Elevation and Latitude

VOCABULARY STRATEGY

The word *firn* comes from a German word meaning "last year's snow." The word *névé* is related to a Latin word meaning "cooled by snow."

How Glaciers Form

Except for bare rock cliffs, a mountain above the snow line is always buried in snow. Great basins below the highest peaks are filled with snow that can be hundreds of meters thick. In these huge snowfields, buried snow becomes compressed and recrystallizes into a rough, granular ice material called **firn** (feern) or névé (nay-VAY).

Reading in mathematics is different from reading in history, literature, or science. A math lesson has few words, but instead illustrates math concepts using numbers, symbols, formulas, equations, diagrams, and word problems. Use the following strategies, and the lesson on the next page, to help you better understand your math textbook.

A Scan the **title** and **headings** to see which math concepts you will learn about.

B Look for **goals, objectives** or **key ideas**. These help focus your reading.

C Read **explanations** carefully. Sometimes a concept is explained in more than one way to make sure you understand it.

D Look for **special features** such as study or technology tips or connections to real life. These provide more help or information.

E Study any **worked-out solutions** to sample problems. These are the key to understanding how to do the homework assignment.

 MARK IT UP Use the strategies above and the mathematics lesson on the next page to answer these questions.

1. What is this lesson about? _____

   _using scientific notation_____

2. Put a star next to the goals of the lesson.

3. Underline the definition of scientific notation.

4. Circle the explanations of how to rewrite numbers in decimal form.

5. What practical application does scientific notation have in the real world?

   It is used to describe and solve problems that involve large numbers, such as the amount

   of water annually discharged by the Amazon River.

8.4

What you should learn

GOAL 1 Use scientific notation to represent numbers. ★

GOAL 2 Use scientific notation to describe **real-life** situations, such as the price per acre of the Alaska purchase in **Example 6**.

Why you should learn it

▼ To solve **real-life** problems, such as finding the amount of water discharged by the Amazon River each year in **Example 5**.

Scientific Notation A

GOAL 1 USING SCIENTIFIC NOTATION

A number is written in **scientific notation** if it is of the form $c \times 10^n$, where $1 \le c < 10$ and n is an integer. C

⬤ **ACTIVITY**

Developing
Concepts

Investigating Scientific Notation

❶ Rewrite each number in decimal form.

    a. 6.43×10^4 **b.** 3.072×10^6 **c.** 4.2×10^{-2} **d.** 1.52×10^{-3}

❷ Describe a general rule for writing the decimal form of a number given in scientific notation. How many places do you move the decimal point? Do you move the decimal point left or right?

EXAMPLE 1 *Rewriting in Decimal Form*

Rewrite in decimal form.

    a. 2.834×10^2 **b.** 4.9×10^5 **c.** 7.8×10^{-1} **d.** 1.23×10^{-6}

SOLUTION E

  a. $2.834 \times 10^2 = 283.4$ Move decimal point right 2 places.

  b. $4.9 \times 10^5 = 490,000$ Move decimal point right 5 places.

  c. $7.8 \times 10^{-1} = 0.78$ Move decimal point left 1 place.

  d. $1.23 \times 10^{-6} = 0.00000123$ Move decimal point left 6 places.

EXAMPLE 2 *Rewriting in Scientific Notation*

  a. $34,690 = 3.469 \times 10^4$ Move decimal point left 4 places.

  b. $1.78 = 1.78 \times 10^0$ Move decimal point 0 places.

  c. $0.039 = 3.9 \times 10^{-2}$ Move decimal point right 2 places.

  d. $0.000722 = 7.22 \times 10^{-4}$ Move decimal point right 4 places.

  e. $5,600,000,000 = 5.6 \times 10^9$ Move decimal point left 9 places.

Reading an Application

To get a part-time job or to register for summer camp or classes at the local community center, you will have to fill out an application. Being able to understand the format of an application will help you fill it out correctly. Use the following strategies and the sample on the next page to help you understand any application.

A **Begin at the top.** Scan the application to understand the different sections.

B Look for special **instructions for filling out** the application.

C Note any **request for materials** or **special information** that must be included with the application.

D Watch for **sections you don't have to fill in** or **questions you don't have to answer.**

E Look for **difficult or confusing words** or abbreviations. Look them up in a dictionary or ask someone what they mean.

▌▌▌MARK IT UP⟩ Use the warranty application on the following page and the strategies above to answer the questions.

1. Why is it important to fill out and mail this warranty application?

The completed warranty serves as confirmation of ownership in the event of theft and

guarantees that the customer receives special offers and benefits.

2. Underline the phrase that tells when the application must be mailed.

3. What information about the product do you have to supply?

date of purchase and retail price

4. Circle the part of the application that you do not have to fill out.

5. What purchase document must you use to fill out this application?

sales receipt

6. ASSESSMENT PRACTICE Circle the letter of the correct answer.
What amount should you include in the box marked "retail price paid"?

A. the total amount you paid for the product

B. the total amount you paid minus the cost of the maintenance agreement

C. the price marked on the product

D. the cost of extra charges, such as delivery and installation

A Congratulations on investing in a Morel product. Your decision will reward you for years to come. Please complete your Warranty Registration Card to ensure that you receive all the privileges and protection that come with your purchase.

Your completed Warranty Registration Card serves as confirmation of ownership in the event of theft.

Returning the attached card guarantees you'll receive all the special offers for which your purchase makes you eligible.

DETACH AND MAIL PORTION BELOW.

USA Limited Warranty Registration	
123456 XXXX	**ABCDEFG7654321**
MODEL NUMBER	SERIAL NUMBER

Registering your product ensures that you receive all of the benefits you are entitled to as a Morel customer. Complete the information below in ink, and drop this card in the nearest mailbox.

B **IMPORTANT - RETURN WITHIN TEN DAYS**

Date of Purchase

Your Name
First   Initial   Last

Address
Street   Apt. #

City   State   ZIP Code

C **Retail Price Paid** $ _____ **.00**
(Excluding sales tax, maintenance agreement, delivery, installation, and trade-in allowance.) **E**

D **Your Phone Number** (optional)
Area Code   Phone Number

MOREL

Public notices can tell you about events in your community and give you valuable information about safety. When you read a public notice, follow these tips. Each tip relates to a specific part of the notice on the next page.

A Read the notice's **title,** if it has one. The title often gives the main idea or purpose of the notice.

B See if there is a logo, credit, or other way of telling **who created the notice.**

C Ask yourself, **"Who should read this notice?"** If the information in it might be important to you or someone you know, then you should pay attention to it.

D Look for **contact information** that indicates where to get answers to questions.

 MARK IT UP Use the public notice on the next page and the strategies above to answer the questions.

1. What is the purpose of this notice?

   to encourage people to get flu shots

2. Circle the name of the organization that created the notice.

3. Who does this notice apply to?

   anyone who wants to prevent the flu

4. Make a star next to the contact information.

5. Who should get a flu shot earliest—health care workers or healthy people 50–64 years old?

   health care workers

6. **ASSESSMENT PRACTICE** Circle the letter of the correct answer.
   The best time to get a flu shot is
   A. your doctor's decision
   B. October or November
   C. October
   D. December

A When should *YOU* get your flu shot?

C	OCT | NOV	DEC or later
People at high risk of severe illness ✓ **65 years old or older**—Even in you're in great health ✓ **Children 6–23 months old**—Children younger than 2 years old have one of the highest rates of hospitalizations from influenza ✓ **Adults and children with a chronic health condition**—Such as heart disease, diabetes, kidney disease, asthma, cancer, and HIV/AIDS ✓ **More than 3 months pregnant during flu season**—Typically November through March	**Best Time**	**Not too late!**
People who can give the flu to those at high risk ✓ **Household contact or caregiver of someone at high risk** ✓ **Health care workers** ✓ **Household contact or caregiver of a child under 2 years old**—Infants younger than 6 months old can't get a flu shot, but they can get the flu	**Best Time**	**Not too late!**
Your child's very first flu shot ✓ **Children 6 months–8 years old** getting the very first flu shot need a booster shot one month after the first dose of vaccine	**Best Time**	**Not too late!**
Healthy people 50–64 years old	**Best Time**	**Not too late!**
Anyone who wants to prevent the flu	**Best Time**	**Not too late!**

A flu shot is your best protection against the flu.

For more information: Ask your health care provider or call the CDC Immunization Hotline.

English: 1-800-232-2522 ★ Español: 1-800-232-0233   www.cdc.gov/nip/flu D

 B

SAFER • HEALTHIER • PEOPLE

Fight the Flu

Reading a Web Page

When you research information for a report or project, you may use the World Wide Web. Once you find the site you want, the strategies below will help you find the facts and details you need. Look at the sample Web page on the right as you read each of the strategies.

A Notice the page's **Web address,** or URL. Write down the Web address or bookmark it if you think you might return to the page at another time or if you need to add it to a list of sources.

B Read the **title** of the page. The title usually tells you what topics the page covers.

C Look for **menu bars** along the top, bottom, or side of the page. These guide you to other parts of the site that may be useful.

D Notice any **links** to other parts of the site or to related pages. Links are often highlighted in color or underlined.

E Many sites have a link that allows you to **contact** the creators with questions or feedback.

F Use a **search feature** to find out quickly whether the information you want to locate appears anywhere on the site.

MARK IT UP Look at the Web page on the right. Then use the information from the Web page and the tips above to answer the questions.

1. Circle the Web address of this site.

2. Draw boxes around two places you can search the site to see if it contains the information you need.

3. What is the name of the president of QN? _Estelle Beauvais_

4. Put a star by the link you should click on to make an online contribution to QN.

5. **ASSESSMENT PRACTICE** Circle the letter of the best answer.
   This site is designed to give information about
   A. issues of interest to people in Quebec
   B. education in Quebec
   C. raising children in Quebec
   D. politicians people in Quebec should vote for

Q-Net

| Back | Forward | Reload | Home | Images | Print | Security | Stop | **L** |

Location: http://www.qnet.org A

C About QN   Resource Center   Contact Us E   Search

Quebec Network

B

Policy Issues

Census
Civil Rights
Education
Farm Workers
Foreign Policy
Health
Housing &
   Development
Immigration
Social Security

Press Room

Headline News
Press Releases
Sign Up for
   QN News

Special Events

QN Awards
Quebec D
   Conference

Web site Features

What's New?

learning links

INSTITUTE FOR QUÉBECOIS HEALTH

Affiliate Locator
★

President's Corner
Estelle Beauvais

Quick clicks

QN Mission
Job Opportunities
President's Bio

Support QN
Join Online

Web site Search
F
The Archives

Reading Technical Directions

Reading technical directions will help you understand how to use the products you buy. Use the following tips to help you read a variety of technical directions.

A Look carefully at any **diagrams** or **other images** of the product.

B **Read all the directions** carefully at least once before using the product.

C Notice **headings** or **lines** that separate one section from another.

D Look for **numbers, letters,** or **bullets** that give the steps in sequence.

E Watch for **warnings** or **notes** with more information.

 MARK IT UP Use the above tips and the technical directions on the next page to help you answer the following questions.

1. What kind of battery do you need for the clock?

   a 1.5 volt battery

2. How do you know if the time displayed is AM or PM? Circle the answer on the next page.

3. Underline the steps to follow in setting the alarm.

4. How long will the alarm sound if you don't turn it off?

   60 seconds

5. **ASSESSMENT PRACTICE** Circle the letter of the correct answer.
   Which of the following is NOT a safe place to set up the clock radio?
   A. on a stable, flat desk
   B. in the bathroom
   C. away from open windows
   D. on a bedside table

Alarm Clock Radio
INSTRUCTIONS FOR USE

1. SNOOZE/LIGHT BUTTON
2. FUNCTION SWITCH
3. BAND SWITCH
4. TUNING CONTROL
5. VOLUME CONTROL
6. TIME/ALARM SET SWITCH
7. BATTERY DOOR (RADIO)
8. HOUR BUTTON
9. MINUTE BUTTON
10. EJECT BUTTON
11. BATTERY HOLDER (CLOCK)

BATTERIES
FOR RADIO:
To insert batteries, remove the BATTERY DOOR (7) and insert 2 AAA batteries, observing the correct position of the polarity.

FOR CLOCK:
Pull out the BATTERY HOLDER (11). Use a 1.5 volt battery and place with positive electrode facing front. Reinsert battery holder.

C HOW TO PLAY THE RADIO
- Press the EJECT BUTTON (10) to open lid.
- Turn the FUNCTION SWITCH (2) TO "ON" position.
- Use the BAND SWITCH (3) to select broadcasting band (AM or FM).
- Turn the TUNING CONTROL knob (4) to select the listening station.

D TO SET THE TIME
- Slide the TIME/ALARM SET SWITCH (6) to the "T.SET" position.
- Depress the HOUR BUTTON (8) until the correct hour is displayed. Be careful to set time to AM or PM as required. When PM time is registered, a "P" will apppear on the display.
- Depress the MINUTE BUTTON (9) until the correct minute is reached.

TO SET THE ALARM
- Slide the TIME/ALARM SET SWITCH (6) to the "AL.SET" position. "AL" indicator will appear on the display.
- Depress the HOUR BUTTON (8) until the desired alarm hour is displayed. Be careful to correctly set alarm to AM or PM as required. When PM time is registered, a "P" will appear on the display.
- Depress the MINUTE BUTTON (9) until the desired alarm time is reached.

WAKE TO ALARM
- Set the FUNCTION SWITCH (2) TO "ALARM" position. When the desired alarm time is reached, you will hear a sequential "BEEP" alarm for 60 seconds.
- To shut the alarm off temporarily, press the SNOOZE/LIGHT BUTTON (1) once. The alarm will stop for 4 minutes, then come on again.
- To stop the alarm completely, set the FUNCTION SWITCH (2) to "OFF" position.

WAKE TO MUSIC
- Set the FUNCTION SWITCH (2) TO "AUTO" position.
- The radio will turn on automatically at your desired alarm time.

SAFETY PRECAUTIONS E
- Do not place the unit near a moisture environment, such as a bathtub, kitchen, sink, etc. The unit should be well protected from rain, dew, condensation, or any form of dampness.
- Do not place the unit on surfaces with strong vibration. Place the unit only on flat, stable, and level surfaces.

Product Information: Directions for Use

Many of the products you buy come with instructions that tell you how to use them correctly. Directions for use may appear on the product itself, on its packaging, or on a separate insert. Learning to read and follow directions for use is important for your safety. As you read each strategy below, look at the sample.

A Read any **headings** to find out what kinds of information are given with the product.

B Read the **directions**, which usually tell you *why, how, when,* and *where* to use the product, *how much to use, how often,* and *when* to stop using it.

C Carefully read any **warnings** given with the product. The manufacturer will usually tell you what to do if you experience any problems.

D Look for any **contact information** that tells you where to call or write if you have a question about the product.

Solution of Hydrogen Peroxide 3% U.S.P.

Active ingredient: Hydrogen peroxide 3% **A**

Inactive ingredients: 0.001% Phosphoric Acid as a stabilizer and purified water

Indications: For topical use to help prevent infection in minor cuts, burns, and abrasions, or to cleanse the mouth.

Directions: Apply locally to affected areas. To cleanse the mouth, dilute with an equal amount of water and use as a gargle or rinse. Do not use in excess of ten consecutive days. **B**

Warnings: **C**

• FOR EXTERNAL USE: Topically to the skin and mucous membranes. KEEP OUT OF EYES.

• If redness, irritation, swelling, or pain persists or increases or if infection occurs, discontinue use and consult a physician.

• KEEP THIS AND ALL DRUGS OUT OF THE REACH OF CHILDREN. **In case of accidental ingestion, seek professional assistance or contact a Poison Control Center immediately**.

Storage: Keep bottle tightly closed and at controlled room temperature 59°–86° F (15°–30° C). Do not shake bottle.

Questions? (888) 555-1234 **D**

MARK IT UP Use the product directions to help you answer these questions.

1. How do you use the product to cleanse your mouth? _____
mix it with an equal amount of water and use as a gargle or rinse

2. Circle the active ingredient in this product.

3. What should you do if someone accidentally swallows this product? Underline the answer.

4. Draw a box around the number you should call if you have questions about the product.

5. ASSESSMENT PRACTICE Circle the letter of the correct answer.
When should you stop using this product?
A. when the temperature drops below 59° F
B. if pain and swelling increase
C. if you have a minor abrasion
D. ten days after you buy it

Reading a Bus Schedule

Knowing how to read a bus schedule accurately can help you get where you need to go—on time. Look at the sample bus schedule as you read the tips below.

A Look at the **title** to know what the schedule covers.

B Identify **labels** that show **dates** or **days of the week** to help you understand how the daily or weekly schedule works.

C Look at **place labels** to know what stops are listed on the schedule.

D Look for **expressions of time** to know what hours or minutes are listed on the schedule.

E Pay attention to the **organization** of the information. Read across the row to see when a bus will reach each location.

A Route 238   Quincy Center Station - Holbrook/Randolph Commuter Rail Station via Crawford Sq.

WEEKDAY MORNINGS **B**

C Leave Quincy Station	Leave S. Shore Plaza	Leave Crawford Square	Arrive Holb./Rand. Commuter Rail Sta.	Leave Holb./Rand. Commuter Rail Sta.	Leave Crawford Square	Leave S. Shore Plaza	Arrive Quincy Station
D 5:25A	5:43A	5:58A	...	6:25A	6:29A	6:42A	7:08A
6:10	6:28	6:43	6:47A	6:50	6:54	7:07	7:35
6:25	6:43	6:58	7:03	7:20	7:25	7:38	8:06
6:45	7:03	7:19	7:24	7:50	7:55	8:08	8:36
7:05	7:25	7:41	7:46	8:25	8:30	8:43	9:11 **E**
7:30	7:50	8:06	8:11	8:55	9:00	9:13	9:41
7:55	8:15	8:31	8:36	9:25	9:30	9:46	10:14
8:15	8:35	8:51	8:56	10:05	10:10	10:26	10:54
9:10	9:30	9:46	9:51	11:00	11:05	11:21	11:49
10:05	10:25	10:41	10:46				
10:55	11:15	11:31	11:36				

▌▌**MARK IT UP**⟩ Use the bus schedule and the strategies on this page to answer the following questions.

1. Circle the name of one stop on this route.

Students should circle Quincy Station, S. Shore Plaza, Crawford Square, or Holb./Rand.

Commuter Rail Station.

2. What time does the last bus leave Quincy Station for Holb./Rand. Commuter Rail Station on weekday mornings?

_10:55 AM_

3. If you took the 7:25 AM bus from Crawford Square, when would you arrive at Quincy Station?   _8:06 AM_

4. ASSESSMENT PRACTICE Circle the letter of the correct answer. If you have a 10:15 meeting at S. Shore Plaza on Tuesday, what's the latest bus you can take from Holb./Rand. Commuter Rail Station?

A. 8:25   **B.** 8:55   **C.** 9:25   **D.** 10:05

Test Preparation Strategies

In this section you'll find strategies and practice to help you with many different kinds of standardized tests. The strategies apply to questions based on long and short readings, as well as questions about charts, graphs, and product labels. You'll also find examples and practice for revising-and-editing tests and writing tests. Applying the strategies to the practice materials and thinking through the answers will help you succeed in many formal testing situations.

Test Preparation Strategies

You can prepare for tests in several ways. First, study and understand the content that will be on the test. Second, learn as many test-taking techniques as you can. These techniques will help you better understand the questions and how to answer them. Following are some general suggestions for preparing for and taking tests. Starting on page 206, you'll find more detailed suggestions and test-taking practice.

Successful Test Taking

 Study Content Throughout the Year

1. **Master the content of your class.** The best way to study for tests is to read, understand, and review the content of your class. Read your daily assignments carefully. Study the notes that you have taken in class. Participate in class discussions. Work with classmates in small groups to help one another learn. You might trade writing assignments and comment on your classmates' work.

☑ **Reading Check** In what practical way can your textbook help you prepare for a test?

2. **Use your textbook for practice.** Your textbook includes many different types of questions. Some may ask you to talk about a story you just read. Others may ask you to figure out what's wrong with a sentence or how to make a paragraph sound better. Try answering these questions out loud and in writing. This type of practice can make taking a test much easier.

3. **Learn how to understand the information in charts, maps, and graphic organizers.** One type of test question may ask you to look at a graphic organizer, such as a spider map, and explain something about the information you see there. Another type of question may ask you to look at a map to find a particular place. You'll find charts, maps, and graphic organizers to study in your textbook. You'll also find charts, maps, and graphs in your science, mathematics, literature, and social studies textbooks. When you look at these, ask yourself, What information is being presented and why is it important?

4. **Practice taking tests.** Use copies of tests you have taken in the past or in other classes for practice. Every test has a time limit, so set a timer for 15 or 20 minutes and then begin your practice. Try to finish the test in the time you've given yourself.

5. Talk about test-taking experiences. After you've taken a classroom test or quiz, talk about it with your teacher and classmates. Which types of questions were the hardest to understand? What made them difficult? Which questions seemed easiest, and why? When you share test-taking techniques with your classmates, everyone can become a successful test taker.

Use Strategies During the Test

1. Read the directions carefully. You can't be a successful test taker unless you know exactly what you are expected to do. Look for key words and phrases, such as *circle the best answer, write a paragraph,* or *choose the word that best completes each sentence.*

2. Learn how to read test questions. Test questions can sometimes be difficult to figure out. They may include unfamiliar language or be written in an unfamiliar way. Try rephrasing the question in a simpler way using words you understand. Always ask yourself, What type of information does this question want me to provide?

3. Pay special attention when using a separate answer sheet. If you accidentally skip a line on an answer sheet, all the rest of your answers may be wrong! Try one or more of the following techniques:

- Use a ruler on the answer sheet to make sure you are placing your answers on the correct line.

- After every five answers, check to make sure you're on the right line.

- Each time you turn a page of the test booklet, check to make sure the number of the question is the same as the number of the answer line on the answer sheet.

- If the answer sheet has circles, fill them in neatly. A stray pencil mark might cause the scoring machine to count the answer as incorrect.

4. If you're not sure of the answer, make your best guess. Unless you've been told that there is a penalty for guessing, choose the answer that you think is likeliest to be correct.

5. Keep track of the time. Answering all the questions on a test usually results in a better score. That's why finishing the test is important. Keep track of the time you have left. At the beginning of the test, figure out how many questions you will have to answer by the halfway point in order to finish in the time given.

☑ Reading Check What are at least two good ways to avoid skipping lines on an answer sheet?

Understand Types of Test Questions

Most tests include two types of questions: multiple choice and open-ended. Specific strategies will help you understand and correctly answer each type of question.

A **multiple-choice question** has two parts. The first part is the question itself, called the stem. The second part is a series of possible answers. Usually four possible answers are provided, and only one of them is correct. Your task is to choose the correct answer. Here are some strategies to help you do just that.

1. Read and think about each question carefully before looking at the possible answers.

2. Pay close attention to key words in the question. For example, look for the word *not*, as in "Which of the following is not a cause of the conflict in this story?"

3. Read and think about all of the possible answers before making your choice.

4. Reduce the number of choices by eliminating any answers you know are incorrect. Then, think about why some of the remaining choices might also be incorrect.

   • If two of the choices are pretty much the same, both are probably wrong.

   • Answers that contain any of the following words are usually incorrect: *always, never, none, all,* and *only.*

5. If you're still unsure about an answer, see if any of the following applies:

   • When one choice is longer and more detailed than the others, it is often the correct answer.

   • When a choice repeats a word that is in the question, it may be the correct answer.

   • When two choices are direct opposites, one of them is likely the correct answer.

   • When one choice includes one or more of the other choices, it is often the correct answer.

   • When a choice includes the word *some* or *often*, it may be the correct answer.

   • If one of the choices is *All of the above*, make sure that at least two of the other choices seem correct.

   • If one of the choices is *None of the above*, make sure that none of the other choices seems correct.

An **open-ended test item** can take many forms. It might ask you

☑ Reading Check What words in a multiple-choice question probably signal a wrong answer?

to write a word or phrase to complete a sentence. You might be asked to create a chart, draw a map, or fill in a graphic organizer. Sometimes, you will be asked to write one or more paragraphs in response to a writing prompt. Use the following strategies when reading and answering open-ended items:

1. If the item includes directions, read them carefully. Take note of any steps required.

2. Look for key words and phrases in the item as you plan how you will respond. Does the item ask you to identify a cause-and-effect relationship or to compare and contrast two or more things? Are you supposed to provide a sequence of events or make a generalization? Does the item ask you to write an essay in which you state your point of view and then try to persuade others that your view is correct?

3. If you're going to be writing a paragraph or more, plan your answer. Jot down notes and a brief outline of what you want to say before you begin writing.

4. Focus your answer. Don't include everything you can think of, but be sure to include everything the item asks for.

5. If you're creating a chart or drawing a map, make sure your work is as clear as possible.

☑ **Reading Check** What are at least three key strategies for answering an open-ended question?

Reading Test Model
LONG SELECTIONS

DIRECTIONS Following is a selection about the French king Louis XIV, "The Sun King." Read the passage carefully. The notes in the side columns will help you prepare for the types of questions that are likely to follow a reading like this. You might want to preview the questions on pages 135–136 before you begin reading.

The Sun King

It was 1643. King Louis XIII had just died, and his five-year-old son ascended the throne. Over the next 54 years, Louis XIV would become the most powerful ruler in France's history. Because he believed that all power radiated from him, he was called the Sun King. In fact, he thought he and France were one. "*L'état, c'est moi,*" (I am the state) he boasted.

Mazarin Rules No five year old, even the Sun King himself, was capable of running a country, however. The true ruler of France during the boy's youth was the prime minister, Cardinal Mazarin. By ending the Thirty Years' War, Mazarin made France the most powerful country in Europe. He lost support at home, though, by strengthening the central government and raising taxes.

These domestic policies affected the French nobles particularly, and they rebelled. They rioted throughout the country and threatened the young king's life. As a result, Louis vowed to become so strong that no one could threaten him again.

READING STRATEGIES FOR ASSESSMENT

Look for the main idea of the article. What does the author want you to learn about and remember when you have finished reading?

Identify causes and effects. How did rebellions by the nobles affect the young Louis? Why?

Louis Takes Over Louis got his chance when Mazarin died in 1661. He was still only 23 years old, but knew his own mind. "The scene has changed," he proclaimed. He decided to rule without a prime minister and immersed himself in every detail of the government—from the food that was served at his table to the movement of his troops on the battlefield. He described his view of his role in a letter to his son:

> *In a well-run state, all eyes are fixed upon the monarch alone. . . . Nothing is undertaken, nothing is expected, nothing is done except through him alone.*

Not surprisingly, one of his first acts was to bar the nobles from his councils. This weakened their power and brought the government more under the direct control of the king. Louis also gave more power to the government agents who collected taxes and administered justice—and who reported directly to him.

The Economy Booms Although Louis held the reins of government tightly, he did rely on advisers in certain areas. His minister of finance, Jean-Baptiste Colbert, led the way in directing France's economic growth. Colbert tried to keep money in the country by building France's manufacturing industries. He did this by giving money and tax breaks to manufacturers and by putting high taxes on imported goods. Under Colbert's guidance,

Pay attention to passages set off from the text. This indented passage is a quotation from Louis XIV. What does it tell you about his role as king?

Note supporting details. What actions did Colbert take to support France's manufacturing industries?

Louis encouraged his subjects to migrate to the French colony in Canada. There, they could bolster the economy by trading in furs.

The King Lives Well Louis XIV did everything on a grand scale. Although he was only 5 feet 5 inches tall, he seemed much taller because he had excellent posture and held himself with dignity. The high-heeled shoes that he often wore also helped.

The king surrounded himself with luxury. He had a staff of nearly 500 cooks, waiters, and other servants just to keep him well fed. At one meal, he reportedly ate four servings of soup, a whole pheasant, a partridge in garlic sauce, two slices of ham, hard-boiled eggs, a salad, a dish of pastries, and fruit. With an appetite like that, it's a wonder he wasn't as wide as he was tall!

To make sure the nobles did not rebel against him as they had done when he was a child, Louis kept hundreds of them at his palace. They competed to have the honor of waiting outside his bedroom and of being one of the four privileged to help him dress. While away from their homes, the nobles also had less influence over the people—increasing the king's power even more.

Focus on topic sentences. Usually the first sentence of a paragraph, a topic sentence tells you what the paragraph is about.

Culture Flourishes If Louis XIV was the sun around which all France revolved, the palace he had built at Versailles was its shining glory. It stretches for about 500 yards, has approximately 2,000 rooms, and is surrounded by 15,000 acres of woods and gardens dotted with 1,400 fountains. A huge statue of the king looks over the massive courtyard. One of the palace's most magnificent rooms is the Hall of Mirrors. Around about 240 feet long and 40 feet high, it has 17 gigantic windows that look out on the garden. A mirror directly across from each window reflects the view and makes the room seem twice as large. The palace was a showcase for the king's wealth and power and made him the envy of all Europe.

Louis used the palace as a showcase for other arts, especially ballet and opera. Not content to be just a patron, he also participated, actually dancing the title role in the ballet *The Sun King*.

Louis Wages War To keep France the most powerful European state, Louis XIV waged many wars to gain territory from Spain and England. The French people suffered greatly as a result, both in taxes to support the army and in lives lost in battle.

In 1700, the king of Spain died, leaving Spain's throne to Louis's 17-year-old grandson, Philip. This effectively united France and Spain, the two greatest European states. Much of Europe banded together to oppose these two countries in the 12-year War of the Spanish Succession. The war finally ended with a treaty that left Philip as king of

Draw conclusions. What does this information suggest about Louis XIV's character?

Make predictions. How do you think the French people would react to their suffering under Louis XIV?

Spain, but kept France and Spain as separate monarchies.

Realizing that his wars and extravagant spending had almost ruined France, Louis XIV died, sad and sorry, in 1715. The Sun King was gone, but the French people would soon rise from the darkness in a revolution that would change the world.

Now answer questions 1–6. Base your answers on the selection "The Sun King." Then check yourself by reading through the Answer Strategies in the side columns.

ANSWER STRATEGIES

1. Which pair of words best describes Louis XIV?
   A. artistic and shy
   B. generous and self-confident
   C. strong and vain
   D. aggressive and thrifty

Read the answers carefully. Some answers include one word that describes King Louis XIV. Look for the answer in which both words describe him.

2. Which of the following statements best expresses the main idea of this selection?
   A. Louis XIV totally identified with France and was its most powerful ruler.
   B. Louis destroyed the country by his lavish lifestyle and costly wars.
   C. Under the Sun King's rule, France's economy and arts blossomed.
   D. Louis XIV became a great king to make up for being very short.

Look for the main idea. Remember that the main idea of the selection expresses the point of the whole passage, not just part of it.

3. What is the primary reason that Louis built his magnificent palace at Versailles?
   A. to keep the nobles occupied so they wouldn't interfere in the government
   B. to provide employment for French bricklayers, gardeners, servants, and cooks
   C. to keep French money in the French economy
   D. to show off his wealth and success to the other heads of Europe

Reread the selection. In this case, all the answers are mentioned in the passage about Versailles. Reread it to determine which reason was the most important.

4 Which of the following did NOT motivate Louis to become an all-powerful king?

A. his inner strength and confidence

B. rebellions by the nobles when he was young

C. his father's weakness

D. the belief that a successful state required a powerful ruler

5 What effect did Louis XIV's wars have on the French people?

A. They angered the nobles and led to widespread riots.

B. They left many dead and burdened the survivors with heavy taxes.

C. They caused many citizens to immigrate to Canada.

D. They created national pride as the French became the envy of all Europe.

6 What legacy did Louis XIV leave the French people?

> **Sample short response for question 6:**
>
> Louis XIV left the French people a mixed legacy. When he died, France was the most powerful country in Europe. Manufacturing had boomed and the economy had grown.
>
> Louis had also expanded France's territory by fighting many wars. However, because he believed "L'état, c'est moi," he spent money extravagantly on himself while the French people lived in poverty and died on the battlefields. After his death, they would revolt.

Reading Test Practice
LONG SELECTIONS

DIRECTIONS Now it's time to practice what you've learned about reading test items and choosing the best answers. Read the following selection, "They Don't Serve Fries with That." Use the side columns to make notes as you read the passage, focusing on: important ideas, comparisons and contrasts, causes and effects, difficult vocabulary, interesting details, questions you have, predictions you make, and conclusions you draw.

They Don't Serve Fries with That

When you think of French food, what comes to mind? If you're like most American teenagers, you probably said French fries. In fact, though, the *French* in the name refers not to the country where fries were invented, but to the way the potatoes are cut. Many people seem to agree that this worldwide favorite was first created in Belgium. So now you know what French food isn't. Let's take a look at what it is.

Beginnings of Haute Cuisine French food is no ordinary collection of calories. It is so special that it goes by the name *cuisine*, which in French means "kitchen," "cooking," and "cookery" as well as just "food." With the added adjectives *haute* ("high") or *grande* ("noble"), you get the idea that this food does more than just fill your stomach.

Haute cuisine originally was for the upper class and royalty. It differed from the food eaten by the peasants and bourgeois because it required expensive, high quality ingredients, a long time to prepare, and was served and eaten elegantly. It was brought to France in the early 16th century by the Italian noblewoman Catherine de Médicis. She introduced rare and expensive foods such as artichokes, truffles, and ice cream. The whole purpose of cooking became to bring out the natural flavor of foods and blend them to delight the eye as well as the taste buds.

Fancy dishes, glasses, and decorations were created to highlight the food, and table manners improved, too. One innovation—the fork—came into common use during the reign of Louis XIV, the extravagant Sun King.

Precision and Creativity Creating haute cuisine is a precise operation, and actually is as much a science as an art. Dishes are even named based on their ingredients or appearance. To us, for example, all edible hot liquids are just *soup*, but the French distinguish them as *consommé* (clear), *potage* (thick), or *crème* (cream).

Only the freshest ingredients go into haute cuisine. Fortunately, modern-day France has excellent farmland and good transportation so there's no problem getting meats, eggs, dairy products, vegetables, and fruits that are in perfect condition. Ingredients like wine and cheese that are best when aged are also available at their peak of perfection.

The methods of handling and preparing these high-quality ingredients are also specifically spelled out. What proportions of ingredients do you use? At what temperature do you cook them and for how long? How does roasting differ from braising and sautéing? Haute cuisine chefs have all the answers.

They also have plenty of room to express their creativity and artistry, though. Chefs try new combinations, add a pinch of this or a dash of that, and even tinker with the traditional cooking methods. Some experiments may fail, but others may improve the taste of a dish, cut the cooking time, or create totally new dishes.

Stocks and Sauces Traditional or not, all haute cuisine is based on cooking liquids called stocks. In fact, the French refer to them as *fonds de cuisine* or "the foundations of cooking." To make stocks, haute cuisine chefs spend hours browning bones, poultry, or fish in the oven. They then add carrots, onions, and herbs and simmer the mixture in water. As it simmers, they keep skimming off the fat, until it boils down to a fraction of its original volume. Only then is it ready to use for preparing or seasoning other foods.

One of the most important uses of stocks

is in making sauces. There are hundreds of French sauces, but, luckily, they can be grouped into broad categories. Three major categories are white, brown, and hollandaise. Each type of sauce has different ingredients and goes with different foods. Here are examples of each type and how they are prepared and served:

- White sauces—*béchamel, velouté, mornay, suprême*—Mix butter and flour; can add milk, cheese, herbs, or wine. Serve with poultry, fish, veal, or vegetables.
- Brown sauces—*ragoût, diable, piquant*— Simmer meat stock many hours and thicken with flour and milk cooked to turn brown; can add giblets, pickles, or spices. Serve with red meat, poultry, veal, or game.
- Hollandaise sauces—*béarnaise, mousseline*— Mix lemon juice and melted butter with warmed egg yolks; can add whipped cream, herbs, or wine. Serve with fish, eggs, or vegetables.

Nouvelle Cuisine and Beyond Traditional haute cuisine sticks to guidelines like these for making sauces. Since it is an art as well as a science, though, French cooking continues to change. One development is appropriately named *nouvelle* ("new") *cuisine*. It does away with thickened sauces and uses small portions of foods in unusual combinations.

Today, you can sample this new French cooking at restaurants across America and around the world. Tomorrow, who knows what heights haute cuisine will rise to? You can bet, though, that whatever form it takes, it won't include a side of fries.

Now answer questions 1–6. Base your answers on the selection "They Don't Serve Fries with That."

1 What is the author's main purpose in this selection?

A. to persuade readers to eat French food

B. to describe French haute cuisine

C. to compare haute cuisine and *grande cuisine*

D. to explain why people shouldn't eat French fries

2 Which of the following is NOT a goal of haute cuisine?

A. enhancing foods' natural flavors

B. pleasing peoples' eyes and stomachs

C. smothering foods in sauces

D. blending fresh ingredients that go together well

3 Where did haute cuisine begin?

A. in Belgium

B. in the Alps

C. in France

D. in Italy

4 How does *nouvelle cuisine* differ from haute cuisine?

A. It is made from fresher ingredients.

B. It uses smaller portions, more unusual combinations, and no thickened sauces.

C. It involves not cooking foods as slowly to keep in their flavors.

D. It is more expensive.

5 Why are stocks so important in haute cuisine?

   A. They are used in making all sauces and in cooking other foods.

   B. They take a long time to cook so people develop a good appetite.

   C. They can be made from anything—bones, meat, poultry, fish, or vegetables.

   D. They provide the money needed to pay for it.

6 What are some advantages and disadvantages of haute cuisine?

THINKING IT THROUGH

The notes in the side columns will help you think through your answers. See the answer key at the bottom of the next page. How well did you do?

1 What is the author's main purpose in this selection?

> Notice that answer choices C and D are based on misreadings of the selection. You can also eliminate the answer that may be the author's underlying purpose, but is not the main one.

- **A.** to persuade readers to eat French food
- **B.** to describe French haute cuisine
- **C.** to compare haute cuisine and *grande cuisine*
- **D.** to explain why people shouldn't eat French fries

2 Which of the following is NOT a goal of haute cuisine?

> Read the question carefully, paying special attention to the word printed in capital letters.

- **A.** enhancing foods' natural flavors
- **B.** pleasing peoples' eyes and stomachs
- **C.** smothering foods in sauces
- **D.** blending fresh ingredients that go together well

3 Where did haute cuisine begin?

> You can eliminate the answer choice that is not mentioned in the selection and the one that is not associated with haute cuisine. Skim the selection to decide between the other two choices.

- **A.** in Belgium
- **B.** in the Alps
- **C.** in France
- **D.** in Italy

4 How does *nouvelle cuisine* differ from haute cuisine?

> Notice that three of the answer choices include characteristics of haute cuisine that are not discussed about *nouvelle cuisine*.

- **A.** It is made from fresher ingredients.
- **B.** It uses smaller portions, more unusual combinations, and no thickened sauces
- **C.** It involves not cooking foods as slowly to keep in their flavors.
- **D.** It is more expensive.

5 Why are stocks so important in haute cuisine?

  A. They are used in making all sauces and in cooking other foods.

  B. They take a long time to cook so people develop a good appetite.

  C. They can be made from anything—bones, meat, poultry, fish, or vegetables.

  D. They provide the money needed to pay for it.

> Notice that answer choice C is true, but doesn't answer the question. Choice B can't be determined from the information given, and D is based on a different meaning of *stocks*.

6 What are some advantages and disadvantages of haute cuisine?

The main advantage of haute cuisine is that it uses fresh ingredients, which makes it healthy. It also is good to look at as well as to eat. Disadvantages are that you need to be a trained chef to make it right and that it takes a long time to cook. That means that it can't be made at home very easily. Because you have to get it at a restaurant, haute cuisine costs a lot. The fact that it's made from rare and high-quality foods makes it even more expensive.

> This is considered a strong response because it
> - directly addresses the question and stays on the topic.
> - supports statements with details from the selection.
> - draws logical conclusions.
> - is well-organized and clearly written.
> - uses correct grammar, punctuation, and spelling.

**Find the main idea and
supporting details.** Circle the
main idea of the article. Then
underline the details that
support the main idea.

Use context clues. To discover
what a "separatist" is, study the
words and phrases around it.
Which phrase helps define it?

Notice important details.
Underline details that explain
the importance of industry in
Quebec.

Reading Test Model
SHORT SELECTIONS

DIRECTIONS "Canada's Many Cultures" is a short
informative article. The strategies you have just learned
can also help you with this shorter selection. As you read
the selection, respond to the notes in the side column.

When you've finished reading, answer the multiple-
choice questions. Use the side-column notes to help you
understand what each question is asking and why each
answer is correct.

Canada's Many Cultures

Canada's people come from different
cultures, and many wish to safeguard their
special language and customs. Some French-
speaking Canadians are separatists, or
people who want the province of Quebec
to become an independent country. In 1980
and 1995, separatists asked for a vote on
whether Quebec should become independent.
Both times the issue was defeated, but the
separatists promised to try again.

Quebec's Importance The federal
government wants Quebec to remain part
of Canada. Quebec is responsible for half of
Canada's aerospace production, half of its
information technology, and 38 percent of its
high-tech industry. French culture is important
in Canada's history and modern-day identity.

Laws Protecting Multiculturalism The
Quebec provincial government has passed
laws to preserve its citizens' French heritage.
In an attempt to satisfy the separatists,

Canada's federal government passed the Canadian Multicultural Act in 1988. This act guarantees the right of all Canadians to preserve their cultural heritage. Finding ways to maintain a unified country remains a critical issue in Canada today.

1 Which of the following best describes the main idea of the article?

   A. Multiculturalism is important in Canada.

   B. The Canadian government wants Quebec to remain a part of Canada.

   C. People in Quebec speak French.

   D. Separatists do not want Quebec to remain a part of Canada.

> **Identify the focus.** Each answer choice offers information from the article, but only one choice explains what the entire article is about.

2 What law did the Canadian federal government pass in 1988?

   A. The Canadian French Language Act

   B. The French Multicultural Act

   C. The French Heritage Act

   D. The Canadian Multicultural Act

> **Evaluate details.** Think about what country the law affects, and what the subject of the article is. Which answer choice makes the most sense, given these two pieces of information?

3 What do separatists in Quebec want?

   A. Quebec to become an independent country

   B. Quebec to become a province of Canada

   C. Quebec to separate into pieces

   D. Quebec to be governed by separatists

> **Pay attention to the context of unfamiliar words.** Find the sentence in the article where *separatist* is used. Notice that the information needed to make the correct choice can be found right next to the word *separatist* in the article.

Read the title. What does the title tell you the chart is about?

_____

_____

Read the labels. What do the labels on the left side of the chart tell you? What about the labels at the top of the chart?

_____

_____

ANSWER STRATEGIES

> Read the question carefully. Notice that the question asks for the deepest lake, not necessarily the largest.

> Read labels carefully. Make sure you understand which row presents information on Lake Huron.

> Follow rows and columns carefully. If necessary, use your finger to trace across a row or down a column so that you don't accidentally wind up in the wrong place with the wrong information.

Answers:
1. A, 2. D, 3. A, 4. C, 5. D, 6. B

DIRECTIONS Some test questions ask you to analyze a visual rather than a reading selection. Study this chart carefully and answer the questions that follow.

The Great Lakes in Canada

	Surface Area (sq. mi.)	Depth (feet/meters)	Elevation (feet/meters)
Lake Superior	11,100	1,330/405	600/183
Lake Huron	13,900	750/229	579/176
Lake Erie	4,930	210/64	570/174
Lake Ontario	3,880	802/244	245/75

4 What is the depth, in feet, of the deepest lake?

A. 750

B. 570

C. 1,330

D. 802

5 What is the surface area in Canada of Lake Huron?

A. 4,930 square miles

B. 11,100 square miles

C. 1,330 square miles

D. 13,900 square miles

6 At what altitude in meters is Lake Erie?

A. 244 meters

B. 174 meters

C. 183 meters

D. 579 meters

Reading Test Practice
SHORT SELECTIONS

DIRECTIONS Use the following selection to practice your skills. Read the paragraphs carefully. Then answer the multiple-choice questions that follow.

St. Martin: Two Islands in One

The island of St. Martin, one of the Antilles in the Caribbean Sea, is divided into two parts. One part (about two thirds of the island) is French, and one part (about one third) is Dutch. The Dutch call the island by the same name, but spell it differently: Sint Maarten. It is named for Saint Martin of Tours; Columbus sighted the island on the saint's feast day. The original treaty between the two countries was signed in 1648, but it was not until 1817 that the current boundaries were established.

Each side retains its own culture and language, but you don't need a passport to cross from one side to the other, and many people on both sides speak English. Caribbean culture is a strong influence on both sides of the island, and most island-born people speak Creole in addition to English, French, and Dutch. The French side of St. Martin is part of the *département* of Guadeloupe. Fishing and tourism are the main occupations there.

1 What was the author's purpose in writing this selection?

A. to persuade the reader that St. Martin is a great place to visit

B. to inform readers about the island of St. Martin

C. to explain why St. Martin is divided into two parts

D. to describe the history of the island of St. Martin

2 Which of the following is a conclusion you can draw from the selection?

A. The French and Dutch have coexisted peacefully on the island since 1648.

B. France discovered the island first.

C. The boundaries on St. Martin have remained the same since 1817.

D. The official language on both sides of the island is Dutch.

DIRECTIONS Use the graph below to answer the questions that follow.

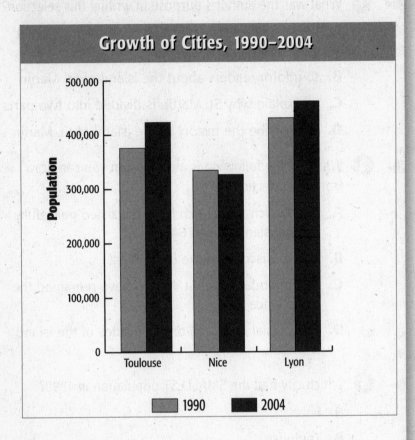

Growth of Cities, 1990–2004

3. Which city had the SMALLEST population in 1990?

   A. Nice

   B. Toulouse

   C. Lyon

4. Which city had the LARGEST population in 2004?

   A. Nice

   B. Toulouse

   C. Lyon

5. Which city had the SMALLEST population increase between 1990 and 2004?

   A. Nice

   B. Toulouse

   C. Lyon

THINKING IT THROUGH

1 What was the author's purpose in writing this selection?

   A. to persuade the reader that St. Martin is a great place to visit

   B. to inform readers about the island of St. Martin

   C. to explain why St. Martin is divided into two parts

   D. to describe the history of the island of St. Martin

2 Which of the following is a conclusion you can draw from the selection?

   A. The French and Dutch have coexisted peacefully on the island since 1648.

   B. France discovered the island first.

   C. The boundaries on St. Martin have remained the same since 1817.

   D. The official language on both sides of the island is Dutch.

3 Which city had the SMALLEST population in 1990?

   A. Nice

   B. Toulouse

   C. Lyon

4 Which city had the LARGEST population in 2004?

   A. Nice

   B. Toulouse

   C. Lyon

5 Which city had the SMALLEST population *increase* between 1990 and 2004?

   A. Nice

   B. Toulouse

   C. Lyon

Answers:
1. B, 2. C, 3. A, 4. C, 5. C

Functional Reading Test Model

DIRECTIONS Study the following nutrition label from a package of chocolate-covered biscuits. Then answer the questions that follow.

Nutrition Facts

Serving Size 2 biscuits (25 g)
Servings Per Container 6

Amount Per Serving	
Calories 125	
Calories from Fat 55	

	% Daily Value*
Total Fat 6 g	10%
Saturated Fat 4 g	20%
Cholesterol 5 mg	2%
Sodium 50 mg	2%
Total Carbohydrate 15 g	
Dietary Fiber 2 g	8 %
Sugars 8 g	
Protein 2 g	

Vitamin A 0% • Vitamin C 0%
Calcium 0% • Iron 0%

* Percent Daily Values are based on a 2,000 calorie diet.

1. How many calories does this whole box of cookies contain?

   A. 825

   B. 750

   C. 700

   D. 800

2. If you ate two servings of cookies, how many milligrams of sodium would you consume?

   A. 50

   B. 75

   C. 100

   D. 200

3. Are chocolate-covered biscuits a smart food choice for people trying to limit their fat intake?

   A. No, because each serving has 6 grams of fat.

   B. Yes, because the serving size is just two cookies.

   C. No, because they have 125 calories per serving.

   D. Yes, because they have 50 milligrams of sodium per serving.

NOTES

READING STRATEGIES FOR ASSESSMENT

Examine the structure of the label. Notice the types of information included in each of the four parts of the label.

Do the math. Remember that the "% Daily Value" and vitamin and mineral numbers on the label are for just a single serving.

ANSWER STRATEGIES

To find the correct answer, multiply the number of calories per serving by the number of servings in the package.

Again, multiplication is the key to finding the correct answer.

To answer this question, just look at the part of the label that tells how much fat each serving contains.

Answers:
1. B, 2. C, 3. A

Functional Reading Test Practice

DIRECTIONS Study the following travel advertisement for a vacation package to Tahiti. Circle the information that you think is most important. Then answer the multiple-choice questions that follow.

EXPERIENCE THE EXCITEMENT OF

TAHITI!

Snorkeling! Windsurfing! Sailing! Golf!
First-Class Entertainment!

4 days/3 nights at the
Tahiti Adventure Resort

only **$689** per person
airfare included *

Adventure Resort Package also includes
continental breakfast, two beach passes,
two spa treatments

*Price based on double occupancy. Airfare from
New York City only. From Chicago add $175. From
Los Angeles add $350. Single travelers add $200.

---

1 Which of the following is NOT included in the $689 price?

    A. beach passes

    B. windsurfing

    C. spa treatments

    D. continental breakfast

2 How much will this vacation package cost a single traveler from Los Angeles?

    A. $479

    B. $1,029

    C. $1,239

    D. $689

3 For which of the following is this vacation package the LEAST expensive per person?

    A. two sisters from New York

    B. a stockbroker from Los Angeles

    C. a single traveler from New York

    D. a college student from Chicago

THINKING IT THROUGH

The notes in the side column will help you think through your answers. Check the answer key at the bottom of this page. How well did you do?

> Although the ad mentions windsurfing prominently, it does not indicate that this activity is included in the price.

1 Which of the following is NOT included in the $689 price?

   A. beach passes

   B. windsurfing

   C. spa treatments

   D. continental breakfast

> To answer this question, read the small type at the bottom of the ad and add the extra charges to the advertised price. Double occupancy means two people staying in the same room.

2 How much will this vacation package cost a single traveler from Los Angeles?

   A. $479

   B. $1,029

   C. $1,239

   D. $689

> Read each answer choice carefully. How many people are traveling? Where are they coming from? Then use the information in the ad to determine who will get the best deal.

3 For which of the following is this vacation package the LEAST expensive per person?

   A. two sisters from New York

   B. a stockbroker from Los Angeles

   C. a single traveler from New York

   D. a college student from Chicago

Revising-and-Editing Test Model

DIRECTIONS Read the following paragraph carefully. Then answer the multiple-choice questions that follow. After answering the questions, read the material in the side columns to check your answer strategies.

¹Paris, the capital of France. ²It is home to one of that nations cultural treasures—the Louvre museum. ³The building was constructed in the thirteenth century as a fortress. ⁴Then they opened it there in 1783 today it has over 500,000 square feet of exhibition space. ⁵The museum is located on a street called the Rue de Rivoli. ⁶Their are many famous works of art they're, including the Venus de Milo and the Mona Lisa.

ANSWER STRATEGIES

1. Which sentence in the paragraph is actually a fragment, an incomplete thought?

    A. sentence 1

    B. sentence 3

    C. sentence 4

    D. sentence 5

> **Incomplete Sentences** A sentence is a group of words that has a subject and a verb and expresses a complete thought. If either the subject or the verb is missing, the group of words is an incomplete sentence.

2. In sentence 2, which of the following is the correct possessive form of the word *nation*?

    A. nation's

    B. nations's

    C. nations'

    D. nations

> **Possessive Nouns** In sentence 2, the word *nation* is singular. So, it takes the singular possessive form.

Pronoun References Avoid unclear or inaccurate pronoun references. In sentence 4, *they* has no antecedent and must be replaced with the noun *government*. The antecedent for *it* is also missing and must be replaced with *first state museum*.

Run-on Sentences A run-on sentence is two or more complete thoughts joined without correct punctuation. Often the word *and* is used instead of a period to connect the two complete thoughts—a clue that the sentence is a run-on.

Spelling Errors Words that sound the same may be spelled differently and have different meanings. Check to be sure that the spelling you use carries the meaning you intend.

Logical Organization The order of the sentences in a paragraph should be logical. The location of the Louvre logically should come before the sentence that discusses the museum's construction.

3 What is the best way to rewrite the first part of sentence 4?

A. Then he decided to change it to an art museum

B. In 1783, the government opened the first state museum there

C. Then in 1783, they made it into the first state museum

D. After a while, they decided to open a big art museum there

4 Which sentence in the paragraph is a run-on sentence?

A. sentence 1

B. sentence 2

C. sentence 4

D. sentence 5

5 What is the best way to rewrite the first part of sentence 6?

A. They're many famous works of art their

B. They're are many famous works of art their

C. There are many famous works of art there

D. Their are many famous works of art there

6 Sentence 5 is out of place. Where should sentence 5 occur?

A. after sentence 2

B. before sentence 2

C. after sentence 6

D. after sentence 3

Answers:
1.A, 2.A, 3.B, 4.C, 5.C, 6.A

Revising-and-Editing Test Practice

DIRECTIONS Read the following paragraph carefully. As you read, circle each error that you find and identify the error in the side column—for example, misspelled word or incorrect punctuation. When you have finished, circle the letter of the correct choice for each question that follows.

¹On May, 22, 1885, one of the most greatest writers in French history died. ²He was born in Besançon. ³As a young man, Victor Hugo writes poetry and helped found a literary magazine. ⁴In 1831 his novel. ⁵*Notre Dame de Paris,* known in English as *The Hunchback of Notre Dame,* was published. ⁶He also wrote many successful plays and other works, he was elected to the *Academie Française* in 1841.

1 Which sentence in the paragraph is a fragment?
- **A.** sentence 2
- **B.** sentence 4
- **C.** sentence 5
- **D.** sentence 6

2 What is the correct way to write the date in sentence 1?
- **A.** May/22/1885
- **B.** May 22 1885
- **C.** May 22, 1885
- **D.** May, 22 1885

3 In sentence 1, which of the following is the correct form of the superlative adjective?

A. greatest

B. greater

C. more great

D. more greatest

4 Which of the following errors occurs in sentence 2?

A. unclear pronoun reference

B. incorrect capitalization

C. incorrect punctuation

D. incorrect verb tense

5 Which of the following is the correct way to rewrite the first part of sentence 3?

A. As a young man, Victor Hugo wrote poetry and helps found

B. As a young man, Victor Hugo is writing poetry and helped found

C. As a young man, Victor Hugo wrote poetry and is helping found

D. As a young man, Victor Hugo wrote poetry and helped found

6 Which of the following is the best way to punctuate the middle of sentence 6?

A. plays and other works, he was elected

B. plays and other works. He was elected

C. plays and other works—and he was elected

D. plays, and other works, and, he was elected

THINKING IT THROUGH

Use the notes in the side columns to help you understand why some answers are correct and others are not. Check the answer key on the next page. How well did you do?

1 Which sentence in the paragraph is a fragment?

A. sentence 2

B. sentence 4

C. sentence 5

D. sentence 6

> Remember that a sentence has a subject and a verb and expresses a complete thought. Which sentence is lacking either a subject or a verb?

2 What is the correct way to write the date in sentence 1?

A. May/22/1885

B. May 22 1885

C. May 22, 1885

D. May, 22 1885

> When writing a date, the name of the month should be spelled out, and the day and year should be separated by a comma.

3 In sentence 1, which of the following is the correct form of the superlative adjective?

A. greatest

B. greater

C. more great

D. more greatest

> A superlative adjective is formed by adding *-est* to the adjective or placing the word *most* before the adjective. Never do both at the same time.

First check to be sure that words are capitalized correctly, that the sentence is punctuated correctly, and that the verb has the same tense as other verbs in the paragraph. Then ask, "Who is *he*?" Unless you can answer that question with a proper name, the pronoun reference is unclear.

Remember that all the verbs in a paragraph should agree—that is, have the same tense. So both verbs in sentence 3 must agree.

Remember that a run-on sentence is two or more complete thoughts joined without correct punctuation. One solution is to create separate sentences.

4　Which of the following errors occurs in sentence 2?

A. unclear pronoun reference

B. incorrect capitalization

C. incorrect punctuation

D. incorrect verb tense

5　Which of the following is the correct way to rewrite the first part of sentence 3?

A. As a young man, Victor Hugo wrote poetry and helps found

B. As a young man, Victor Hugo is writing poetry and helped found

C. As a young man, Victor Hugo wrote poetry and is helping found

D. As a young man, Victor Hugo wrote poetry and helped found

6　Which of the following is the best way to punctuate the middle of sentence 6?

A. plays and other works; and he was elected

B. plays and other works. He was elected

C. plays and other works—and he was elected

D. plays, and other works, and, he was elected

Answers:
1. B, 2. C, 3. A, 4. A, 5. D, 6. B

Writing Test Model

DIRECTIONS Many tests ask you to write an essay in response to a writing prompt. A writing prompt is a brief statement that describes a writing situation. Some writing prompts ask you to explain *what, why,* or *how.* Others ask you to convince someone of something.

As you analyze the following writing prompts, read and respond to the notes in the side columns. Then look at the response to each prompt. The notes in the side columns will help you understand why each response is considered strong.

Prompt A

Some child-rearing experts believe that young people should be kept busy after school and on the weekends with a variety of structured activities, such as music lessons, sports, dance classes, and so on. Others say that young people today have been "overscheduled" and need more time to themselves—to read, think about the future, and even just to daydream.

Think about your experiences and the way your non-school time is structured. Do you think lots of structure, more personal time, or a combination of the two is most beneficial to young people? Remember to provide solid reasons and examples for the position you take.

Strong Response

Today was a typical day for my little brother Jeff. He got up
at five o'clock to go to the local ice rink for hockey practice.
Then he was off to school. At the end of the school day,

ANALYZING THE PROMPT

Identify the focus. What issue will you be writing about? Circle the focus of your essay in the first sentence of the prompt.

Understand what's expected of you. First, circle what the prompt asks you to do. Then identify your audience. What kinds of details will appeal to this audience?

ANSWER STRATEGIES

Capture the reader's interest. The writer begins by describing a typical busy day in his younger brother's life.

Jeff had a piano lesson followed by a meeting of his Cub Scout troop. After a quick dinner, he did homework for two hours. He finally got to bed at ten o'clock. That's a lot to pack into a single day, especially since Jeff is just seven years old! I think that in addition to sports, music, and other activities, kids like Jeff need some time to themselves.

Many parents, mine included, think a busy kid is a safe kid. They believe that the less time a kid has on his hands, the less likely he'll wind up doing something he shouldn't be doing or being with people he shouldn't be with. That's probably true for many kids. After all, it's hard to get into trouble when you spend every day being carpooled from one activity to another.

But some busy kids do get into trouble anyway. Jeff's friend Mark got caught trying to shoplift a CD last weekend, and he's involved in just as many activities as Jeff is. So having a busy schedule is no guarantee that a kid won't get into trouble.

Plus, I think kids benefit from having free time to go to the movies, play video games, read, or even just be by themselves. Growing up isn't always easy, and kids need some time alone to figure things out, think about what's important to them, and decide what they really want to do.

Last Saturday afternoon, Jeff's soccer practice was canceled because of thunderstorms. We went to see a movie and later spent some time talking and listening to music in my room. It was the first time in months that we had time just to hang out together, and we really enjoyed it. Jeff said it was like having a day off. I think more kids like Jeff could use a day off too.

State the position clearly. The last sentence of the first paragraph makes the writer's position clear to the reader. Now the writer can spend the rest of the essay developing his argument.

Address opposing views. The writer brings up an opposing view—that busy kids are less likely to get into trouble—and admits that it might sometimes be true.

Use good examples to support the position. Here, the writer uses an example to make the point that not all busy kids stay out of trouble.

Use logical reasoning to further develop the position. The writer offers logical reasons why free time is important.

Restate the position in the conclusion. Using another concrete example, the writer restates his position that kids need some time to themselves.

Prompt B

Depending on where you live, each season of the year can be very different than it is in other parts of the country. Which season do you enjoy the most—summer, autumn, winter, or spring? What is that season like in your part of the country? What makes it special to you?

Strong Response

Here in the upper Midwest, the seasons seem as different from one another as night and day. Summer usually arrives suddenly. The temperatures soar, the humidity rises, and fierce thunderstorms add drama and sometimes destruction to the season. Autumn brings a crisp, cool, and colorful change as the leaves turn golden and the air turns chilly. Winter can be bitterly cold, and heavy snows often make the simple trip to school a real ordeal.

Then comes spring. Spring is a truly magical time of the year. I can sense spring long before it actually arrives. There's a certain scent in the air, and something is different about the way the sunlight looks. Soon the winter snows are reduced to muddy puddles. The tree branches swell with buds, and the first green shoots of crocus and tulip leaves struggle up out of the ground. Most magical of all, the early morning hours just after dawn are filled with the cries of migrating birds heading back north.

Because my family lives in a small community surrounded by farmland, I get to experience a different kind of spring than many people do. The fields behind our house fill up with wildflowers that season the air with perfume and color. A trip to Jefferson's Pond offers a chance to watch ducks and geese resting on their long

Look for the main idea. The first few sentences of the prompt present the subject you will write about. Try restating the subject in your own words.

Understand what's expected of you. What does the prompt ask you to do? Explain something? Persuade someone? State your personal feelings?

ANSWER STRATEGIES

Create an intriguing introduction. The writer arouses the reader's curiosity by leaving out one of the four seasons.

Include specific details. The writer uses specific details about each season to make the description vivid.

Include the kind of information the prompt asks for. Notice how the writer follows the directions in the prompt by explaining what spring is like in her part of the country.

Use sensory details. Details that appeal to the reader's sense of sight, sound, and smell bring the description to life.

seasonal journeys. The apple and cherry trees at the McKlintock family orchards explode with blossoms until they look like giant balls of cotton candy.

Mostly, however, I love spring because it is a season of hope. The earth is coming back to life, filled with possibilities. I feel like I am, too.

Writing Test Practice

DIRECTIONS Read the following writing prompt. Using the strategies you've learned in this section, analyze the prompt, plan your response, and then write an essay explaining your position.

Prompt C

You have volunteered to participate in your community's semiannual blood drive. Your task is to write a letter to your community newspaper encouraging everyone in town to consider giving blood.

Think about all the ways your community benefits from having an adequate blood supply. Write a letter that explains what these benefits are. Include specific examples. End your letter by appealing to your fellow citizens' sense of civic pride and duty.

Scoring Rubrics

DIRECTIONS Use the following checklist to see whether you have written a strong persuasive essay. You will have succeeded if you can check nearly all of the items.

The Prompt

☐ My response meets all the requirements stated in the prompt.

☐ I have stated my position clearly and supported it with details.

☐ I have addressed the audience appropriately.

☐ My essay fits the type of writing suggested in the prompt (letter to the editor, article for the school paper, and so on).

Reasons

☐ The reasons I offer really support my position.

☐ My audience will find the reasons convincing.

☐ I have stated my reasons clearly.

☐ I have given at least three reasons.

☐ I have supported my reasons with sufficient facts, examples, quotations, and other details.

☐ I have presented and responded to opposing arguments.

☐ My reasoning is sound. I have avoided faulty logic.

Order and Arrangement

☐ I have included a strong introduction.

☐ I have included a strong conclusion.

☐ The reasons are arranged in a logical order.

Word Choice

☐ The language of my essay is appropriate for my audience.

☐ I have used precise, vivid words and persuasive language.

Fluency

☐ I have used sentences of varying lengths and structures.

☐ I have connected ideas with transitions and other devices.

☐ I have used correct spelling, punctuation, and grammar.

Credits

Acknowledgments

"La petite fille" by Topor. © Topor. "Sur le fil à sécher le linge" by Corinne Albaut. © Corrine Albaut. "Mes pantoufles" by Anne-Marie Chapouton. © Anne-Marie Chapouton. "Mère-Mouton" by R. Lichet. © R. Lichet. "Les bonbons" by Topor. © Topor.

Illustrations

MapQuest.com 95

Gary Hincks 97

McDougal Littell/Houghton Mifflin Co.

Photography

23 Parrot Pascal/Corbis Sygma; **93** Lee Foster/Bruce Coleman, Inc.; **97** *left* Galen Rowell/Corbis; *right* David Muench/Corbis; **103** Timothy Fadek/Corbis; **107** Dennis MacDonald/PhotoEdit; **109** 1991 Kathleen Marie Rohr/DDB Stock Photo; **111** School Division/Houghton Mifflin Co.; **113** Jacques Jangoux/Getty Images; **119** School Division/Houghton Mifflin Co.

All other photos by Lawrence Migdale/PIX/McDougal Littell/ Houghton Mifflin Co.